The Theory of Recreational Diving

Prepare for Your Dive Professional Exam,
Be an Informed Recreational Scuba Diver

Marc F. Luxen Ph.D.
Sally Powell

Visit the on-line course at

www.easydivetheory.com

Visit Facebook page of the book and the course at

https://www.facebook.com/easydivetheory?fref=ts

Copyright © 2016 Marc Luxen and Sally Powell.

All rights reserved. This book or any portion thereof may not be reproduced or used in any manner whatsoever without the express written permission of the publisher except for the use of brief quotations in a book review.

For ordering information contact info@easydivetheory.com

ISBN-13:978-1523453672

ISBN-10:1523453672

CONTENTS

Introduction   **6**

   How to use this book and how to study   7

The Diving Environment   **10**

   Tides   10
   Currents   15
   Coasts   19
   Waves   19
   Marine life   25

The Physics of Diving   **30**

   Heat   30
   Light   32
   Sound   36
   Pressure   37
   Ambient pressure, absolute pressure and gauge pressure   38
   The relationship of pressure to the volume and density of a gas (Boyle's Law)   39
   Calculating Volume   40
   Calculating air consumption   42
   Partial Pressure (Dalton's Law)   43
   The relationship of temperature pressure and volume (Charles' Law)   46
   Saturation, super-saturation and excessive super-saturation   48
   Buoyancy   50
   Calculating buoyancy   51

Dive Equipment   **56**

   Tanks   56
   Regulators   60

Depth gauges	63

The Physiology of Diving — *66*

Blood. oxygen, carbon dioxide and carbon monoxide	66
The cardiovascular system	69
Lungs	73
Respiration, oxygen and carbon dioxide	75
The effects of breathing oxygen under pressure	78
Gas narcosis	80
Decompression sickness	81
Risk of decompression sickness	86
Barotraumas	89
Lung over-expansion injuries	89
Ear and sinus barotraumas	92
Temperature problems	95

Decompression Theory — *98*

Half-times	98
Compartments (theoretical tissues)	101
M-values	104
Repetitive Dives	107

Appendix 1 Summary — *110*

The dive environment	*110*
Physics	*111*
Equipment	*112*
Physiology	*113*
Decompression theory	*116*

Appendix 2 Exam and answer key — *118*

Table of Figures — *126*

Index — *128*

INTRODUCTION

Theory of Recreational Scuba Diving: The Dive Environment, Physics, Equipment, Physiology and Decompression theory made easy.
This books tells you exactly what you need to know, not more, not less.
With many illustrations, summaries, links to webpages, and exercises.
For serious divers, dive professionals, and people preparing to become a dive professional.

Welcome to your journey into dive theory. We hope you will enjoy reading about the thing you love: diving. We wrote this book to help you understand what is happening and why it happens before, during, and after a dive. Maybe you will be preparing for an exam to become a dive professional. Maybe you are a serious diver who wants to know more about your favourite hobby. And maybe you are beginning diver who wants to know everything here is to know about diving, at least as much, or preferably more, than your instructor. Buy this book. It teaches you all you need to know, no more, no less. This is book tells you all you need to know, no more, no less. We know that there are more books about dive theory on the market, and many of them are excellent. So why did we write this book? Because we think that other books are too short, too long, too difficult, too easy, tell you too much or tell you not enough. Who do we think we are to say this? Why would you trust us? Good question. First, we are dive professionals ourselves. We worked in many different countries, for many years, with entry level and professional level students, for different dive organisations. We think we know what we are talking about. Marc Luxen has a PhD in psychology with an interest in dive psychology and has lots of experience in writing educational texts. Sally Powell has a MA in graphic design, and has taught and studied teaching the theory of diving intensively for years. We decided we could write a book that might help you. And of course because we thought it would be fun to write it.

We did even more. We made an on-line course with videos and many more exercises to help you study. This is also the place where people all over the world taking this course help each other with questions and answers. Visit the on-line course at

www.easydivetheory.com

You can visit the Facebook page of the book and the course at

https://www.facebook.com/easydivetheory?fref=ts

We will start off easy with a short introduction to the dive environment, where we look at tides, currents, waves, coasts, ecosystems. Why are there usually two tides per day, but only one Moon? Why do currents follow a certain pattern over the globe? What makes waves big, how do they break at the beach? How many different types of coasts are there, and why? How do marine biologists talk about the marine life they study and describe?

Next, we go on with the physics of diving. We will keep the numbers to a minimum, and we promise: no formulas. We will show you how to use your experience as a diver and your common sense to understand and calculate everything. If you have a fear of physics and calculations, as we know many of you have, we will cure you from it. Give it a go. You will calculate buoyancy, air consumption, pressure, and partial pressure with a smile on your face. Well, perhaps that is too much to ask. Without sweating, let's settle for that.

Next, we have a look at equipment, but because manufactures can give you so much more information than we can, and because we know you love shopping or looking at brochures, we keep it to the minimum. We tell you about tanks and tank maintenance, burst disks, balanced and unbalanced regulators, venture valves, pilot valves, up-stream and down-stream valves, and types of depth gauges.

After this, we are ready to understand what happens in your body when you go diving. In the physiology of diving, we will have a look at blood, hearts, lungs, ears, and all the things that can go wrong. More importantly, we will give you the knowledge you need to respond when things go wrong, and even more importantly, how to avoid things going wrong. That does not mean you won't need an Emergency First Responder course. You do, because you need skills and practice. But you will know all you need to know.

Finally, we can bring it together and talk about decompression theory, how tables and dive computers work. You will know how compartments, half times, M-values are used to make models for your tables or computers to keep you safe.

And now you have it all! You know everything you need to know about the theory of diving.

HOW TO USE THIS BOOK AND HOW TO STUDY

The most important thing you must get in your head is: this supposed to be fun. Forget whatever bad experiences you had with bad teachers and bad books, and studying subjects you did not care about. This is different. You DO care about what you are doing here. You WANT to know the things in this book. Do not rush. Take your time. One word, one line, one paragraph, one page, one chapter at a time. Find a place where you feel nice. Bring something to drink, a paper and a pen. Write things down. Draw pictures that help you understand. Write down your own summary for each section, as if you are making a note you can take to an exam. Reward yourself after each section or two sections or whatever with a break or a snack, but never stop in the middle when you are trying to understand something. If you really cannot understand something, write down exactly what you do not understand. Write down your question. Next time, you might understand it, or someone can help you with the answer. Only stop when you have finished something. To help you understand what the most important points are, we give you a short summary after each section called:

Key things to remember

Read them. Check if you understand them without effort. If you want to check if you understood this whole book, just read all these summaries. If you understand them all without any problems, you have understood it all. You have arrived. At the end of the book we put all these sections together, so you have a complete summary, you can use to review things.

A very important tool is the exam with the answer key. We have chosen to use multiple choice questions with only two answer alternatives. That way, we were able to use many questions, covering the complete theory. Every important thing has its own question. This way, you know exactly what you know and what you do not know after making this exam. Questions with two answer alternatives are also harder than questions with four answer alternatives, because, let's face it, usually two of the four answers are obviously bullshit anyway. So this exam is also more difficult than most exams the dive industry commonly uses. If you get it here, you get it everywhere.

There is also an index at the end of this book. You can use this to quickly look up a term you have forgotten or want to read about again. And if you want to know more, as we hope you do, sooner or later, we have given you links to interesting web pages after each section as well. Just follow a link, follow the links in that link, the links in that link of the link, and before you know it, you will be an expert in micro bubbles detection or coastal geography. Or tsunamis. Or Pneumothorax injuries. Or exponential wash-out models with different M-values. Have fun.

Have fun, that last one is so important we will repeat it again. This is about diving! You love this! Enjoy studying this book, do not bring the bad habits and bad attitudes you may have picked up at school or wherever with you. Learning about things you like is one of the nicest things you can do in life. Do not cheat yourself out of the pleasure this book can give you. Good luck. You will do fine, and better than that.

THE DIVING ENVIRONMENT

We are going to look at the Sun, the Moon and how they cause the tides. We will move on to how currents circle Earth, what causes them and how the rotation of Earth influences them. Then we hop onto the land, and have a look at different coasts. Then we get back into the water again, and have a look at winds and waves. Last, you get a short overview of the way marine biologists look at marine life.

TIDES

How the Sun and Moon cause tides. Spring tides, neap tides,
Three patterns of tides caused by the rotation of Earth and topographical features:
Diurnal, Semi-Diurnal and Mixed tides.

The gravity of the Moon and the Sun pull the water in the oceans up, and this is the cause of the tides. How big this pull, the gravity, of a thing like the Moon or the Sun is, depends how heavy it is and how far away it is. The Sun is much heavier than the Moon, but the Moon is much, much closer to us. You will read in many texts that the gravity of the Moon is larger than that of the Sun because it so close to Earth. This is not true. The Sun's pull on Earth is in fact about 175 times larger than the pull of the Moon! But it is true that the Moon that influences the tides the most. This is because tides are caused by the differences in the gravity on different places on Earth. You can visualise this by placing the Moon on one side of Earth in your mind, and keep everything still, no rotation yet! Now, its gravity is different say on the part of Earth facing the Moon, than the part that is on the other side. Have a look at Figure 1. And it is this difference that causes tides. Because the Sun is so far away, these differences are much smaller for the gravity of the Sun. And so, it is the Moon that mainly causes the tides

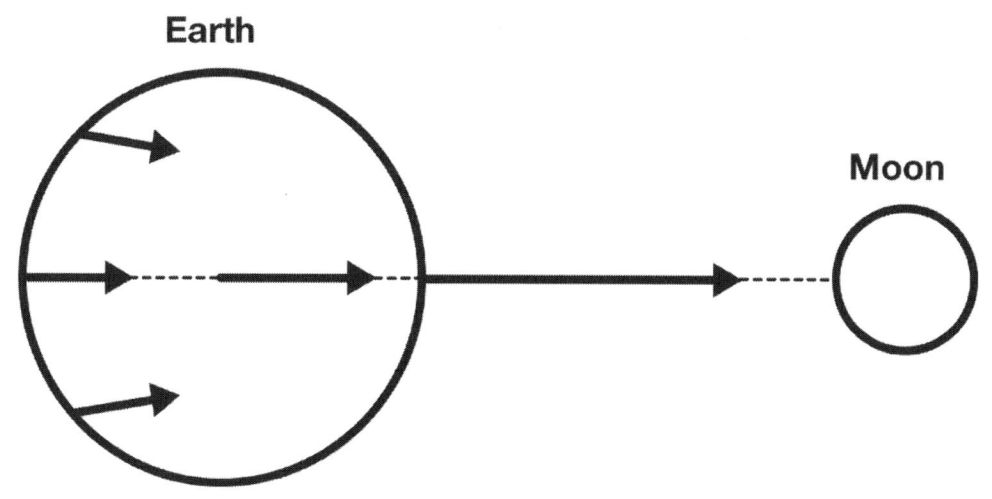

So it is logical to first look at the Moon. To make it simple, imagine that Earth is perfectly round and standing still, and that it is completely covered with water without any land. On the side of Earth where the Moon is hanging (where the gravity is greatest) the water swells outwards. The gravitational field also causes the water on exactly opposite side of Earth to swell outwards, because the pull is the least at that location. You can see it like this: The Moon pulls the water directly underneath it up, and the further away you go from the Moon, the less it pulls. When you are the other side of Earth, the force is gone, and you will have another swell. (Again, many texts explain this wrong. The fact that there are swells on both sides has nothing to do with Earth turning around its own axis, the centrifugal force, as some texts will claim. Do not listen to them). This is hard to imagine, I know. You do not have to understand exactly how and why, but you should understand this: the gravitational pull of the Moon creates two swells in the water of either side of Earth, one where the Moon is, and one on the opposite side (in more technical terms these swells are called bulges, that is term you would mostly see on websites and in books). Can you visualise this? Good, it should look something like Figure 2. Now, because Earth turns, these swells of water move around Earth (or, rather, Earth moves underneath them). You can see this happening in your mind? Now we are finally there: where there is no swell, it is low tide, and where there is a swell, it is high tide

Figure 1 Different gravity force of the moon on different places on earth

The Earth rotates under the bulges.

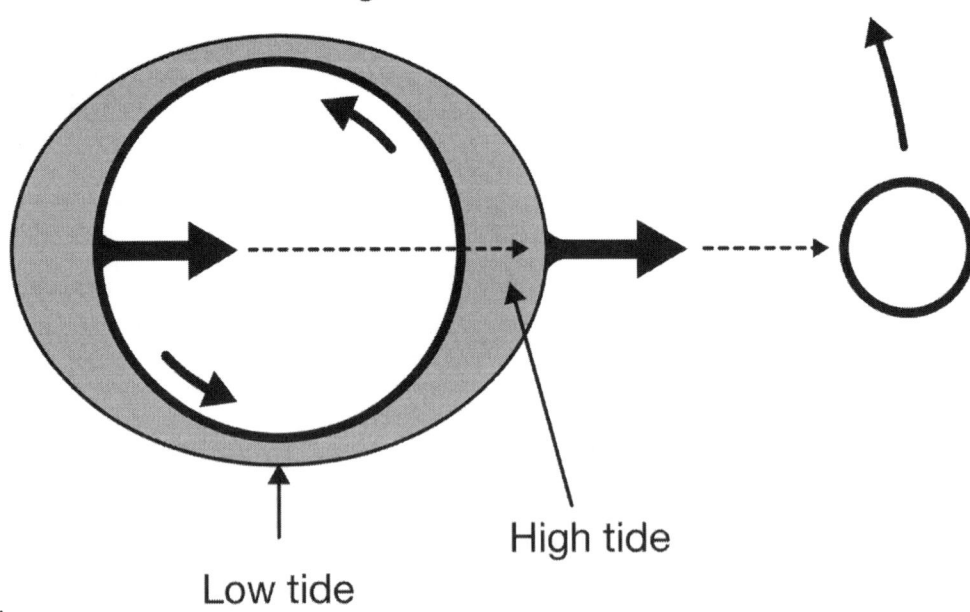

Low tide

High tide

Figure 2 Two bulges of seawater caused by the gravity of the moon

Now that you know the Moon creates two swells in the water on opposite sides of Earth, you may think that there would be a high tide twice a day, and a low tide twice a day. After all, Earth spins in 24 hours around its axis, so you would meet two swells per day. But it is not that simple. First, the shape of the sea bottom. This is called the topographical features of the sea, remember this term. The topographical features affect the amount and duration of the tides. In the middle of the Pacific Ocean, where there is no land, the difference is only a few inches. But in Calais and Dover there is a huge difference between high and low tide (around 15 meters or more), because all the water coming from the open ocean is forced through the narrow funnel of the English Channel between France and England. Second, the rotation of Earth has a direct effect on the tides. The rotation of Earth causes the water in the oceans to move in big slow whirlpools around certain points (if you want to know, these points are called amphidromic points, but you are welcome to forget that, although you might impress people with this knowledge). So, the shape of the sea bottom and the big whirlpools currents disturb our nice simple two-high-tides-two-low-tides picture.

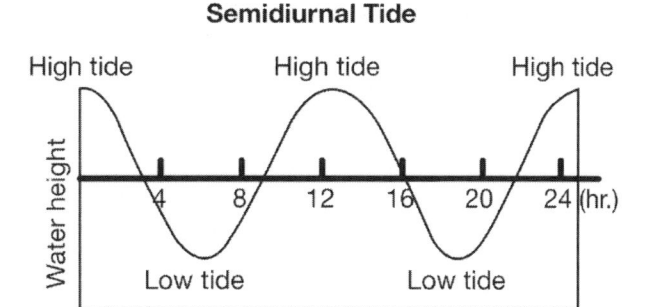

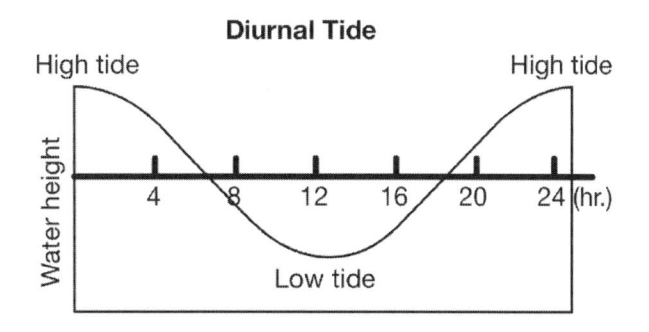

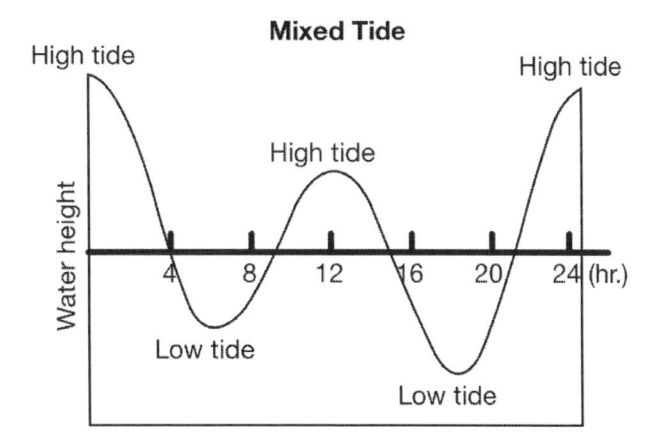

Figure 3 Diurnal, semi-diurnal and mixed tides

There are in fact three different patterns of tides on Earth. First, in some places there are semi-diurnal (that means half-daily) tides: twice daily tides with two high tides equal in height and two low tides equal in height (semi means half and diurnal means daily, so it is a that tide occurs once every half day). Second, in some places there are diurnal (daily) tides: tides that occur once a day.

And third, there are places with mixed tides: twice daily tides with two high tides of unequal heights and two low tides of unequal heights. Yes, you need to know these terms: diurnal tides, semi-diurnal tides, and mixed tides and how they are caused. See Figure 3.

Ok, we have dealt with the Moon. Now let's look at the Sun. The same story is true for the Sun: the gravitational pull creates two swells in the water on either side of Earth.

New Moon - Spring Tide

Full Moon - Spring Tide

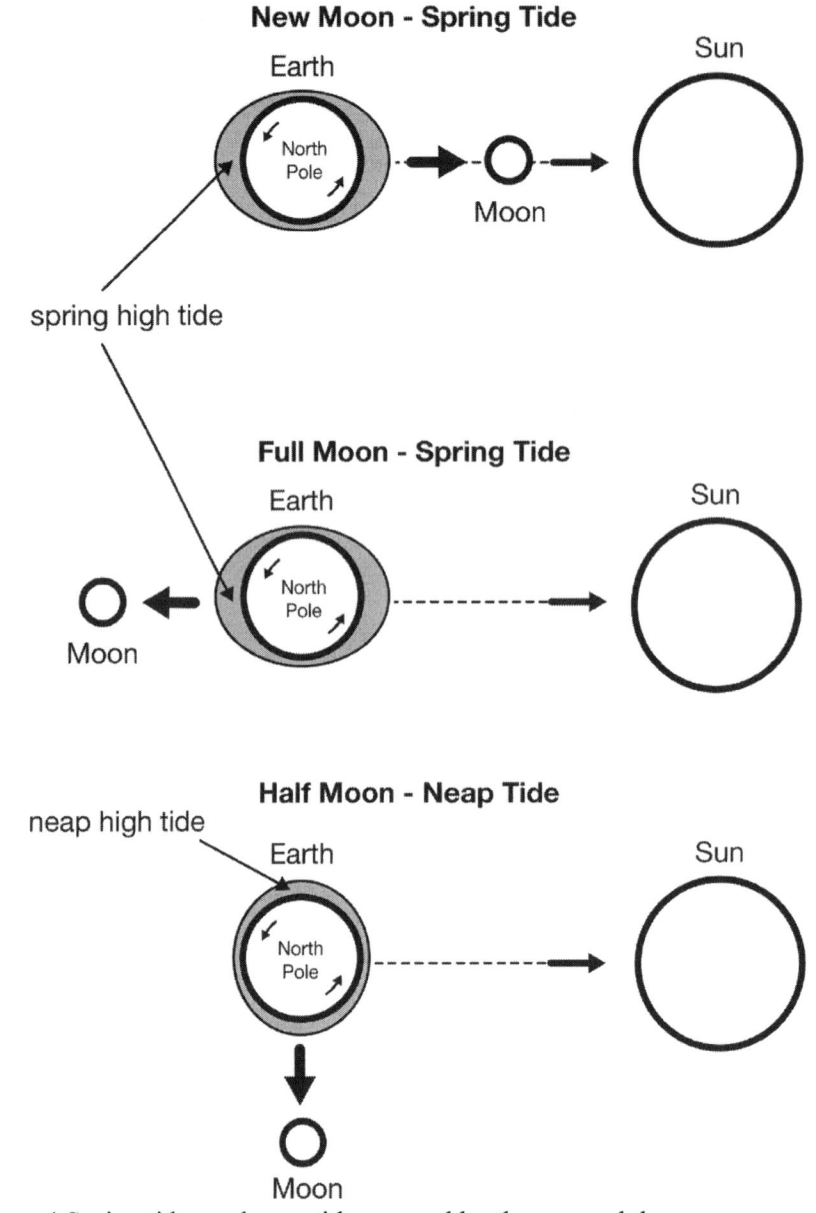

Half Moon - Neap Tide

Figure 4 Spring tides and neap tides caused by the sun and the moon

But because the Sun is much, much, further away than the Moon, the swells it creates are much smaller. We hardly notice them. However, because everything rotates, at certain times in the month the swells created by the Moon and by the Sun align. This alignment happens at what we know as Full Moon (when the Sun and Moon are on opposite sides of Earth and we can see the whole Moon) and at New Moon (when the Moon is directly in front of the Sun and we can barely see the Moon) Have a look at Figure 4 to make these clear. At Full Moon and New Moon the high tides are extra high and the low tides are extra low. We call this a spring tide.

When the Sun and Moon work against each other because they are located at a 90 degrees angle to each other (you can see this in the sky as a Half-Moon), the tidal change is the smallest. This is when there is the least difference between high tides and low tides. We call this a neap tide. So, you need to remember what spring tides and neap tides are, and why they occur.

What does that mean for us divers? Simple: when there is a big difference between a high and low tide there is a lot of water movement, which means that there will be strong currents. You don't want to go diving at those times. In theory, the best time to dive is during slack high tide (the time when the water has reached its highest point before it begins to ebb again) at a Half-Moon, when the tide swells are smallest. Remember this, and remember why this is. Some of your students or buddies might want to know.

Key things to remember:

The pull of gravitational fields of the Moon and the Sun creates tides. Although the Sun is larger, the Moon is much closer and has a larger effect. Because of the influence of land formations and the rotation of Earth, there are three different types of tidal patterns in different places on Earth: semi-diurnal (two high tides and two low tides of equal heights per day), diurnal (one high tide and one low tide per day) and mixed tides (two high tides and two low tides of unequal heights per day). At Full Moon and New Moon the pull of the gravitational fields is strongest and we call this spring tide. Currents are strongest in the water at this time and conditions for diving are less favourable. At Half-Moon the gravitational fields of the Moon and Sun work against each other and we call this neap tide. Currents are generally weakest around this time, meaning that the conditions for diving tend to be better.

Find out more:

http://scienceblogs.com/startswithabang/2010/02/24/how-tides-work

CURRENTS

Currents caused by tides, global wind patterns, and upwellings. Big currents, called gyres, go clockwise on the Northern Hemisphere, and counter-clockwise on the Southern Hemisphere because of the Coriolis Effect.

So now we know that tides cause currents, and when currents are strongest. But tides are not the only causes of currents. The wind also causes big currents at sea. The major winds always blow in the same direction, from the hot equator to the cold poles and back. You would think that these winds go north-south (or south-north on the southern hemisphere). But that would be too easy. They blow in fact but east-west (or west-east). This is because of the rotation of Earth. Earth turns underneath them, just as the case was with the tidal swells. We need to have look at our spinning Earth and use our imagination a bit to understand this. Here we go.

Follow me into space. Look back down on the blue Earth, spinning. We go north, and we look down at the North Pole. Now you can see that Earth is turning counter-clockwise. Get that image in your mind, Earth starting at twelve, to nine, and six, and three and full circle. Now we go to the South Pole. Follow me. Earth still spins the same way. But now we look from the other side! Now it looks from our perspective, that it is going clockwise. If you find this hard to imagine, pick up something round and turn it. Look from the top, and then move your head to the bottom. You can see what happens. Have a look at Figure 5.

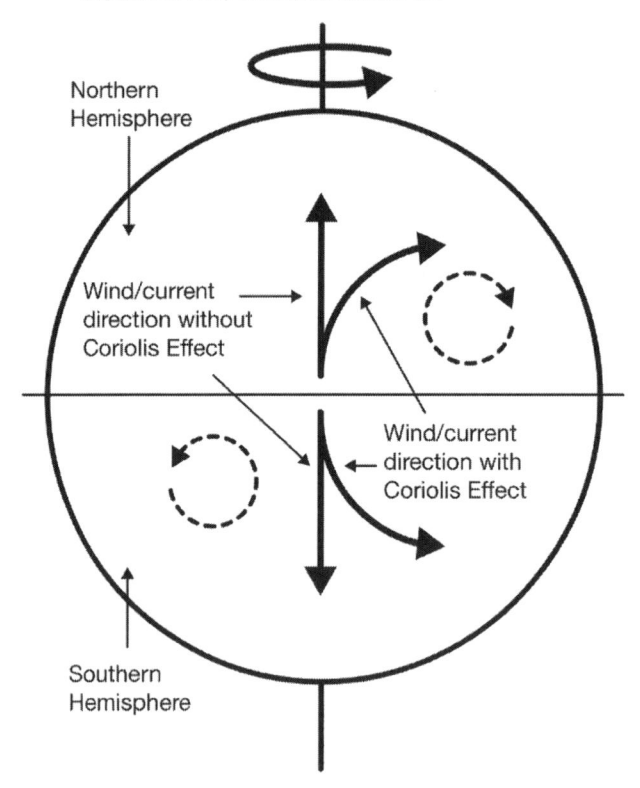

Figure 5 The Coriolis Effect

So, on the northern hemisphere Earth spins counter clock wise, on the southern hemisphere it spins clock wise. Let's go back to Earth. Imagine this: You have a circular piece of paper on a turntable.

Let it spin counter-clockwise, like Earth seen from the North Pole. Now you take a pencil and draw a straight line from the centre of turntable towards you on the paper. Of course, your straight line will not be straight, because the paper is turning. Your 'straight line' will appear to curve to the left or in a clockwise direction (because the paper turns underneath it). Now if you draw your 'straight line' and at the same time rotate the circle clockwise, as if you were looking up at the South Pole, what will happen? The line will curve to the right, or in an anti-clockwise direction. Try it with a paper that you turn around, so you can see this happening

Now you have all the images in your head that you need to understand the directions of the currents by the wind. The wind is the same as your pencil on the spinning paper. In the Northern Hemisphere the rotation of Earth bends the wind to the right, or in a clockwise direction. In the southern hemisphere the wind bends to the left, or in a counter-clockwise direction. This is called the Coriolis Effect, because *Monsieur* Coriolis from Paris described it first (in 1832 if you really must know, and he was talking about water wheels and machines, not the atmosphere). So, the Coriolis Effect is the bending of something that moves over a thing that turns. Have you ever considered that this happens to airplanes too, for instance? Or that hundreds of years ago they corrected for the Coriolis effect when they shooting at each other with cannonballs? So let's summarise for us divers: the Coriolis Effect causes currents to bend to the left, clockwise, the west, on the Northern Hemisphere, and to the right, counter clock wise, the east, on the Southern Hemisphere.

The major ocean currents follow this pattern. These large ocean currents are called gyres. In the Northern Hemisphere the major currents run clockwise, for example: from south to north along the east coast of North America, west to east across the Atlantic, and north to south along the west coasts of Europe and North Africa. In the Southern Hemisphere the major currents run counter-clockwise, for example: from south to north along the coast South Africa, from east to west across the Atlantic and north to south along the coast of South America. So, now you know about currents caused by tides, and currents by global wind patterns (gyres).

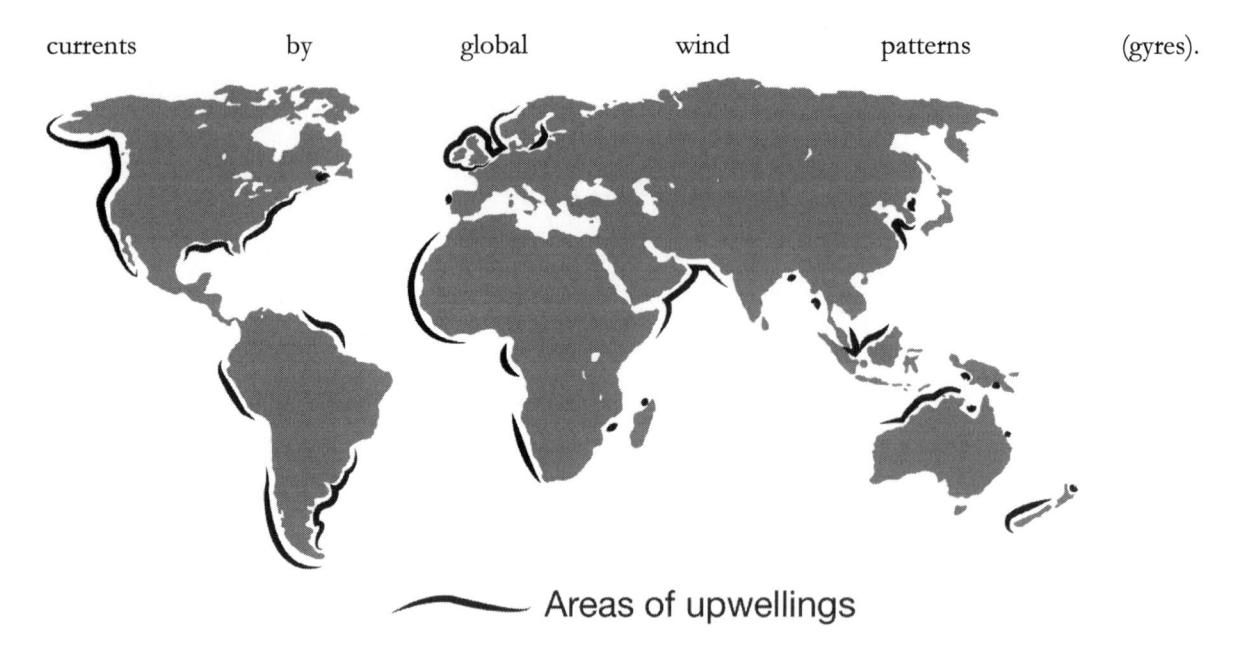

Figure 6 The main upwellings on earth

There is one more cause of currents, but they are thankfully much easier to understand: upwellings. An upwelling occurs when winds that always come mainly from the same direction drive warm surface water away from the shore. This causes cold, nutrient-rich water to rush upwards to take its place, and this causes a current. This usually happens on the west coasts of continents, for example in California, Peru, Canary Islands, and Western Australia. See Figure 6. This is great for divers, although the water is colder. This cold water is full of food such as phytoplankton, and so it attracts many fish and mammals.

Key things to remember:

There are three causes of currents in the sea: 1) currents caused by tides 2) currents caused by global wind patterns 3) currents caused by upwellings. Currents caused by global wind patterns go clockwise in the Northern Hemisphere and counter-clockwise in the Southern Hemisphere. This is due to the rotation of Earth and it is an example of the Coriolis Effect.

Find out more:

http://www.youtube.com/watch?v=QfDQeKAyVag
http://en.wikipedia.org/wiki/Corioliseffect
http://en.wikipedia.org/wiki/Upwelling

COASTS

Primary coasts, made by processes of the land.
Secondary coasts, made by processes of the ocean.

The coast or a coastline is where the sea meets the land. There are many different types of coasts, such as rocky coastlines, beaches, estuaries, coral reefs, and you will probably be able to think of a few other types yourself. Marine scientists call coasts that are created by processes of the land primary coasts. For example, coasts made by volcanoes depositing material, or by glaciers forming fjords, or by rivers depositing materials on the ocean floors and forming deltas, these are all primary coasts. Marine scientists call coasts that are created by processes of the sea itself secondary coasts. For example: coasts made by waves and currents causing erosion or depositing materials, such as beaches, and of course coasts made by the formation of coral reefs. They are called secondary coasts because they are what is left of primary coasts when the sea has destroyed them!

Key things to remember:

A primary coast is one formed by processes of the land, and a secondary coast is one formed by processes of the sea. The type of coast will have a big effect on the type of diving in the area.

Find out more:

http://en.wikipedia.org/wiki/Coast

WAVES

Waves: height, length, frequency and propagation.
Ripples, Seas and Swells.
The fetch and a fully developed sea.
The surf.

You will have noticed of course that when the wind is stronger, the waves are bigger. This is because the waves that you see on the surface of the ocean are actually caused by wind. The wind brushes along the surface, and sweeps the water up. To say this more scientifically: the wind makes waves by transferring some its energy to the water through friction between the air atoms and water atoms. We call these types of waves wind waves (duh) or surface waves (again duh). There is also a type of wave that is not caused by the wind: a Tsunami. This type of wave is caused by underwater Earthquakes, volcanic eruptions and landslides. Tsunamis are sometimes called tidal waves, but this is misleading, because they are not caused by tides. True tidal waves, waves caused by the actual tides do exist, but they are not important to us divers. Let's have a closer look at waves, first look at Figure 7:

- -Waves can be high or low. We call this the wave height: the height from the crests (top) to the troughs (bottom);
- -Wave can be long or short. We call this the wave length: how far apart two crests are from each other;
- -Waves can travel quickly or slowly: we call this the wave speed: how fast the wave is travelling.
- -Waves go in a certain directions: we call this the wave propagation: the direction of the waves;
- -You can have a lot of peaks per second or very few passing by: we call this the wave frequency.

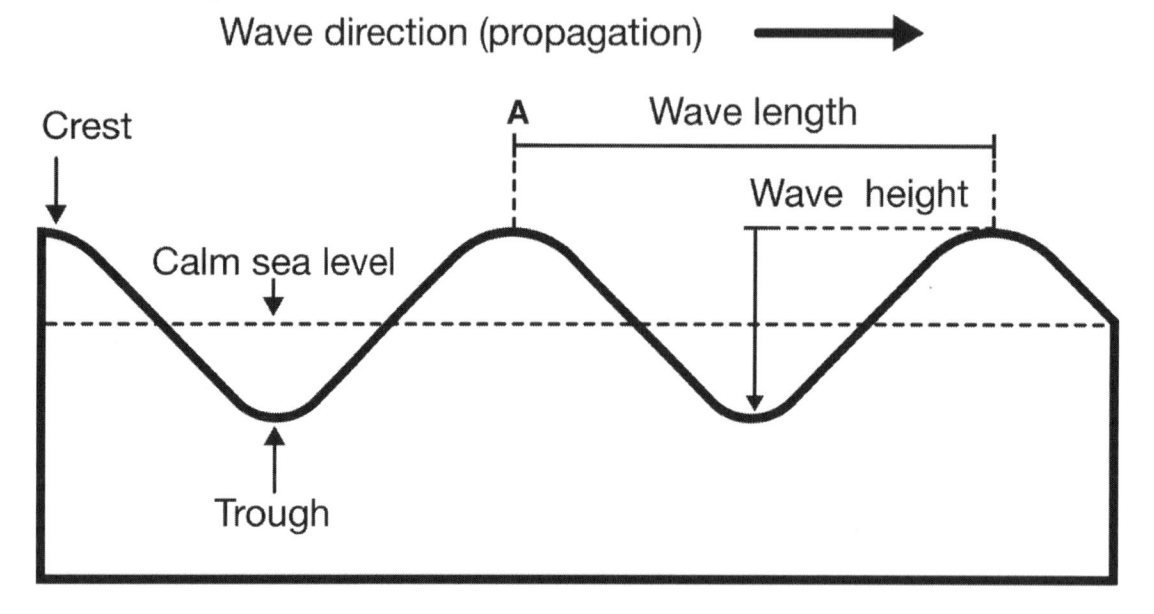

Wave direction (propagation) ⟶

Crest
A   Wave length
Wave height
Calm sea level
Trough

Wave frequency - number of wave crests passing through point A per second.

Figure 7 Wave form: height, length, speed, direction and frequency

The frequency, how many peaks pass per second, depends on how quick the wave goes (wave speed and how close the crests are together (the wave length). Wave Speed, Wave Length and Wave Frequency and are related (and this is how they are related, but you can forget this if you want: Speed = Wavelength x Frequency).

The smallest waves are called ripples, or more scientifically, capillary waves. They have a wavelength of less than 2 cm. They die out quickly when the wind stops, and they are flattened by the surface tension of water. Sailors often call them 'cat's paw' waves because they can look like paw prints. Larger waves are called 'seas' (yes a bit confusing). Seas form if the wind has blown for a long time, and they continue after the wind has died. They are too big to be flattened by surface tension, but they are flattened by gravity. A third and last kind of wave results from seas blending together into groups of common direction and wavelength, and they become very long waves. We call these waves swells. . See Figure 8.

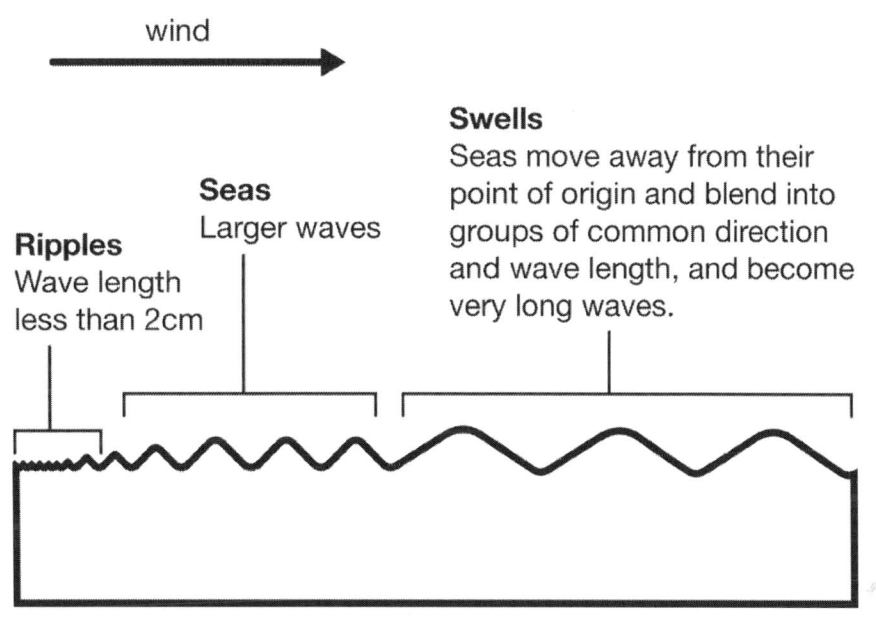

Figure 8 Ripples, seas, and swells

How do wind waves grow? Obviously, the first factor is the wind itself. The more wind, the higher the wind waves can become. And of course the longer the wind blows, the bigger they can become. Furthermore, the longer the stretch of water in the direction of the wind they can grow in, the bigger they can become. This is distance is called the fetch. Thirdly, if the fetch is not only long, but also wide, they can become higher, because the shores do not cause friction. The same goes for the depth of the fetch: the deeper, the less friction. So, wind waves are influenced by the speed and duration of the wind, and the length, width and depth of the water, the fetch. See Figure 9.

This means that waves in a certain area of the sea or a lake (their fetch) can only reach a maximum height. This height is dependent upon the speed of the wind, how long it blows (wind duration) and the fetch (remember that the fetch is the uninterrupted distance of open water over which the wind is blowing). More wind or longer wind does not mean higher waves anymore, because if the waves have reached their maximum height, further exposure to that wind will only cause breaking of wave tops (whitecaps). When this happens, the waves are at their maximum height, and the wind cannot make them higher by blowing faster or longer. We call this a Fully Developed Sea. In the right conditions wavelengths can reach up to 150 km, and a height of 30 metres.

Fetch - the horizontal distance over which the wind blows in a constant direction in an area of water where waves are generated.

Waves reach a maximum height relative to the size of the fetch: the larger the length of the fetch, the larger the waves can be. When waves reach their maximum height we it call it a fully developed sea.

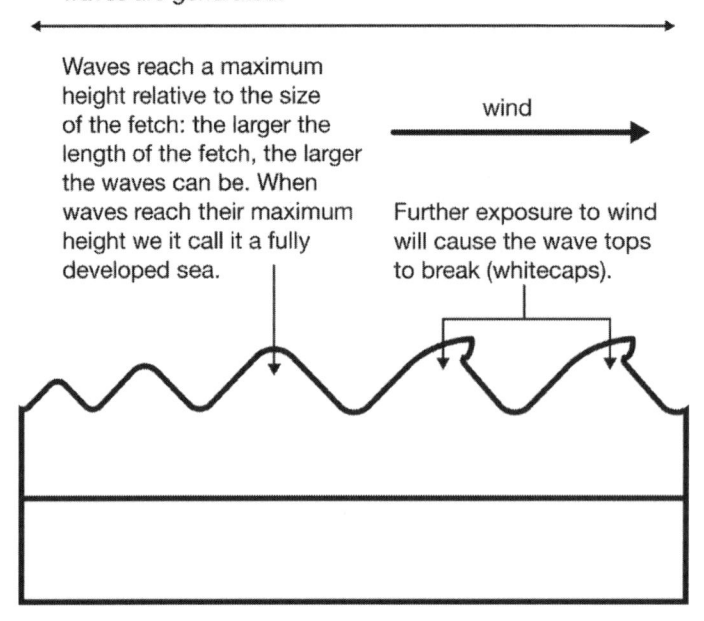

wind

Further exposure to wind will cause the wave tops to break (whitecaps).

Figure 9 Growing of wind waves in the fetch

Quite impressive. But we have not finished yet. Let us have a look what happens when waves start to play together. When waves meet each other they add or subtract the height of their crests. You can imagine that two crests together make an extra high crest, while a crest and trough make a more or less level area of sea, and two troughs make an extra deep trough. This pattern is called interference. When the crests or troughs of two waves cross exactly at the same time and place, and their two heights or depths combine we have constructive interference. When a crest and trough meet, they cancel each other out, and so we call this destructive inference. You can see this happen in Figure 10.

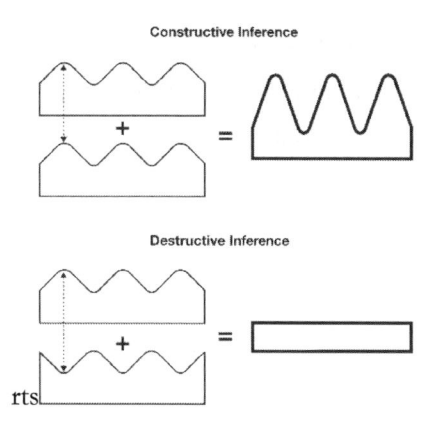

Figure 10 Wave interference: constructive and destructive

You may have heard of mysterious high waves seemingly coming out of nowhere, wrecking ships. These 'rogue waves" or 'freak waves' – are rare waves that are at least twice as high as other waves in the area, and now you can understand that they are mainly the result of constructive interference.

We are still not done talking about waves. Let us leave the water, and stand on the beach. What happens when waves break? Swells from the open sea reach shallower water - this happens at the coastline, but can also happen when waves pass over an obstruction like a sandbar or a reef, and they start breaking. They begin to slow down and their crests and troughs get closer together, just like cars get closer together in a traffic jam. This means that all the energy of the waves gets concentrated in a smaller and smaller area. This energy cannot go anywhere but up, and so waves get higher, while the length of the wave gets smaller. This cannot go on, of course. The front of the swell becomes steeper and steeper, while the back of the wave keeps its rounded shape. Once waves reach water of a depth of about 1.3 times their height, the friction between the front of the wave and the bottom starts to really slow down the front of the wave, while the back of the wave still pushes on, until the back of the wave pushes over the front of the wave, and the wave breaks. Now we have a surf. In Figure 11 you can see how this happens. How quickly the wave breaks depends of course on how steep the sea bottom is: steeper, the quicker the wave breaks.

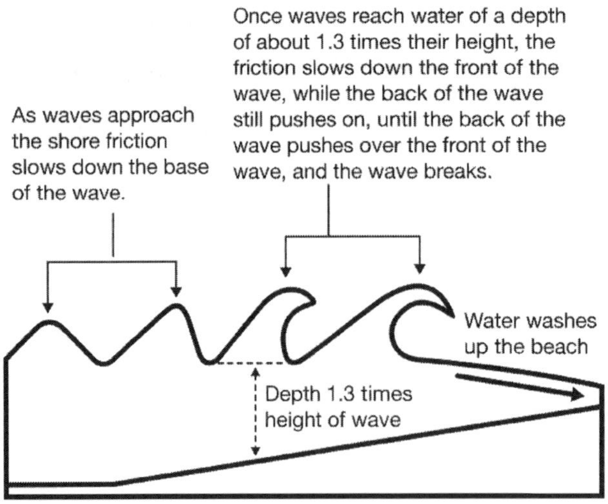

As waves approach the shore friction slows down the base of the wave.

Once waves reach water of a depth of about 1.3 times their height, the friction slows down the front of the wave, while the back of the wave still pushes on, until the back of the wave pushes over the front of the wave, and the wave breaks.

Water washes up the beach

Depth 1.3 times height of wave

Figure 11 Breaking waves in the surf

Key things to remember:

Waves have: 1) the wave height - from crest to trough; 2) the wavelength – distance between two crests; 3) the wave frequency – number of crests per second; 4) the wave propagation (direction); 5) the wave speed. Tsunamis are not caused by the wind, they are caused by underwater Earthquakes, volcanic eruptions and landslides. They are sometimes called tidal waves, but this can be misleading as they are not caused by tides. Five things influence the formation of wind waves: 1) the wind speed; 2) the fetch; 3) the width of the area affected by the fetch; 4) the wind duration; and 5) the water depth. The smallest waves are called ripples or capillary waves (maximum wavelength 2cm). Larger waves are called seas. They separate from their point of origin into swells, whose size is constrained by the wind speed, duration and the fetch. This is a fully developed sea. In shallower water swells slow down, and they become breaking waves when they reach water that is 1.3 times as deep as the height of the wave. They form the surf.

Find out more:

http://en.wikipedia.org/wiki/Wave

http://en.wikipedia.org/wiki/Fetch_(geography)

http://en.wikipedia.org/wiki/Wind_wave

http://en.wikipedia.org/wiki/Breaking_wave

http://en.wikipedia.org/wiki/Constructive_interference

http://en.wikipedia.org/wiki/Rogue_wave

MARINE LIFE

The Benthic, the Pelagic, the Euphotic, the Disphotic and the Aphotic zone.

Ecosystems and the food pyramid/food webs.

Species, Populations, Communities, and Habitats.
Producers, Herbivores, Carnivores and Decomposers.
Symbiosis: Mutualism, Commensalism and Parasitism.

We can really give you only the basics about marine life, but the basics will help you understand what marine biologist are talking about (well, a bit). Let's begin with some of the names that marine scientists use when talking about the ocean.

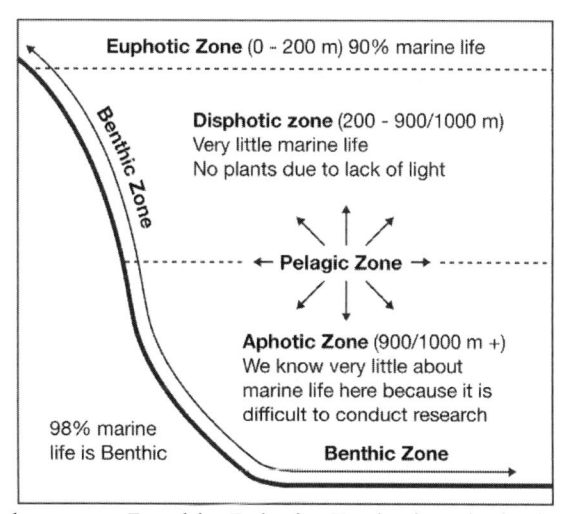

Figure 12 Zones in the ocean: Benthic, Pelagic; Euphotic, Disphotic and Aphotic

The very bottom of the ocean is called the benthic zone. The benthic zone extends from the coastline all the way to the deepest parts of the ocean floor. Everything above the ocean floor is called the pelagic zone. We call anything that spends its life on the bottom of the ocean a benthic organism, and anything that spends its life in the water column a pelagic organism. Scientists think that 98 percent of all marine species are benthic organisms. More than 90 percent of marine life, whether benthic or pelagic, lives in the area near the surface where light can reach. We call this area the euphotic (Greek meaning good light) zone. The area beginning at around 200 metres where the light is poor is called the disphotic (meaning low or poor light) zone. Only approximately 1 percent of sunlight reaches here. And then the area beginning at around 900-1000 metres where no light can reach is called the aphotic (meaning no light) zone. You can see all this in Figure 12.

The aphotic zone makes up 90 percent of the ocean. There is almost no energy there, and that means almost no marine life. Therefore, the majority of marine life lives in only 10 percent of the ocean. No plants can live below the euphotic zone because there is not enough light for photosynthesis to take place. But there still is life below the euphotic zone, because dead organic matter from above sinks down and feeds organisms in the disphotic and aphotic zones. Small fish, jellyfish, squid and simple shellfish can live in the disphotic zone because of this. A sinking wale carcass can mean years of food, of course! Many organisms in this zone have large eyes to help them see, and many are also bioluminescent, meaning that they can make their own light. Some organisms also survive by spending daylight hours in the disphotic zone, and swimming up at night to the euphotic zone to feed (at night there are less predators there). Deeper still, in the aphotic zone where there is eternal darkness, we once thought there was no life. We were wrong, as usual, and that is about all we know. Because it is hard to conduct research there, we know very little about life there.

Now that we have looked at the different zones where they all live, let's have a look that the marine life itself. The word ecosystem means the system of relationships between organisms and their environment in a particular area. You could talk about a marine ecosystem, a jungle ecosystem, a mountain ecosystem or many others. Ecology simply means the study of ecosystems, but sometimes people mean ecosystem when they say ecology.

Within the ecosystem there are species, populations and communities. A species is a group of related individual organisms that have the same characteristics or qualities, and who can breed with each other but not with members of other species. For example angelfish are one species. A population is all of the individuals of a given species in a specific area at a certain time. For example all the angelfish at a particular coral reef are a population. And a community means all the populations in a specific area at a certain time. For example all the organisms, angelfish, stag coral, nudibranches and whatever more is left at a particular coral reef are a community. Within a community, species work together, eat each other, and share places. The place where a particular species lives (or wants to live, or lives best) is called its habitat. This term can be used to refer to a very large area or small area, dependent on the context in which you are talking. You could say that an angelfish's habitat is the ocean, as opposed to the land. Or you could be more specific and say that an angelfish's habitat is a shallow coral reef.

Back to the ecosystem. If you look at how organisms live in an ecosystem by what they eat, you discover that it is a sort of pyramid, with a broad base and a small top (Figure 13). The broad bottom layer of the ecosystem pyramid is where the most organisms (or rather the most weight, the most "biomass") is located. It consists of organisms that make their own food by using energy from the Sun (or very, very rarely by using energy from deep sea volcanic hot spray holes). In the sea these organisms are all plants and algae. We call these organisms primary producers. Without them the ecosystem could not exist, because they are the only ones who provide the energy (food) for the layers on top of them. The main primary producer of the sea is phytoplankton. ('Phyto' means plant and 'plankton' means drifting. So, phytoplankton is plant-like organisms that passively float in the sea). They are too small to be seen with the naked eye, but when they are present in large enough numbers the water may appear to be green. Phytoplankton only lives in the euphotic zone because it needs sunlight for photosynthesis and to produce food.

Straight above the primary producers are organisms that eat them: the plant eaters or as they are called herbivores (you can remember this by thinking that they are voracious for herbs) such as molluscs, krill, sea urchins, the green sea turtle and some small fish, such as surgeonfish. And what also feeds on the primary producers is zooplankton ('zoo' means animal, so zooplankton is passively floating animals. As with phytoplankton, they are usually microscopic).

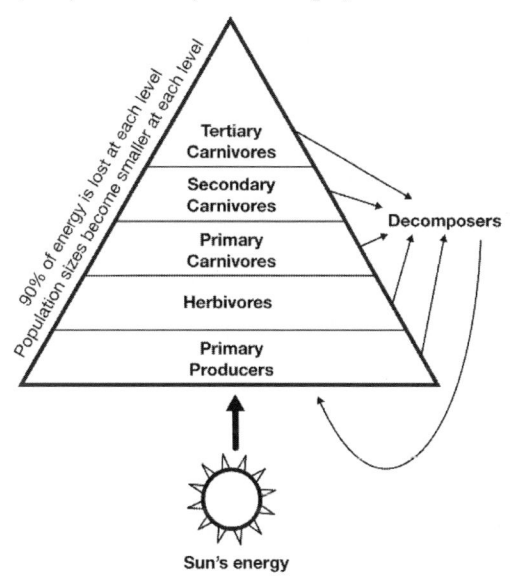

Figure 13 The ecosystem as a pyramid

Of course, some things likes to eat the herbivores. We are now at the third level of the pyramid. This is the first time when animals eat other animals: the carnivores (carne- means meat). Here we find the first, the primary, carnivores. These include squid and some fish, such as angelfish and butterfly fish. You guessed, they get eaten, one level up again, by the, you guessed that too, the secondary carnivores, who eat (yes you guessed it) the primary carnivores. Secondary carnivores include organisms such as sea bass (so you can see size does not matter here, really). And again, secondary carnivores get eaten by tertiary carnivores like barracuda and sharks for example on level 4. How far does this go on? Well, how many levels there are in a pyramid varies, but it is rare that there are more than five levels. This is because a lot of energy gets lost from one level to the next. At each step 90% of the energy is lost. This is why hunting sharks, for instance, is so damaging to ecosystems: it takes enormous amounts of energy to make and support them. If you want to be nice to the world, eat organisms coming from the lower levels of the pyramid.

Now, a pyramid a bit of a simplistic way to represent an ecosystem. Things do not go neatly from level to level. Many organisms are omnivores: they eat plants as well as animals. And there is yet another group of organisms that belongs to an ecosystem, they are called the decomposers. Decomposers are the cleaners in the ecosystem. They live off the waste of other organisms – excrement and dead bodies. Fungi and bacteria are decomposers, Decomposers do an important job because they recycle, keeping the nutrients moving back into an ecosystem. So, it is not really right to think of a pyramid or a food chain, a term you have no doubt often heard too. It is better to think of an ecosystem is as a food web, with links up and down, left and right. But the pyramid image gives you a good idea how things work, more or less. Sorry that the world is complicated!

So far, we have only talked about predator-prey relationships, about who eats who, but that is not the only way organisms interact together, fortunately. Sometimes, things can be nice too. Some species benefit from other species without eating each other. We call these type of relationships symbiotic relationships (the word comes from the Greek 'sym' meaning with, and 'bios' meaning life, so the 'state of living together. There are three types of symbiotic relationships: 1) mutualism, where both organisms benefit from each other; 2) commensalism, where only one organism actually benefits from the relationship, but the other organism is not harmed; 3) parasitism, where one organism benefits from the relationship, and in doing so harms the other organism (ok that is not so nice after all).

Google the following examples of symbiotic relationships to find out more: examples of mutualism are coral and zooxanthellae (a type of algae), the goby fish and pistol shrimp, and cleaner wrasse and various reef fishes; examples of commensalism are sharks/big fish and remoras, turtles and barnacles, anemone fish and anemones (you will hear many people say that this is mutualism, but the anemone doesn't really benefit), Portuguese man-of-war jellyfish and man-of-war fish, and the imperial shrimp and sea cucumber; most examples of parasitism involve organisms that live inside of other organisms, such as parasitic worms living in the intestines of whales, and toxoplasmosis that has been found in sea otters. Marine parasites can be very small, but they are present in huge numbers and put together they can weigh more than all the big predators in an ecosystem together.

Key things to remember:

The very bottom of the ocean is called the benthic zone. We call anything above that the pelagic zone. 98% of marine organisms live in the benthic zone. The first 200 metres (approximately) of the ocean where light can reach is called the euphotic zone. From 200 metres to 900-1000 metres where only 1 percent of sunlight reaches is called the disphotic zone. From 1000 metres where no light can reach is called the aphotic zone. The aphotic zone makes up 90 percent of the ocean, but 90 percent of marine organisms live where light can reach. An ecosystem is the system of relationships between organisms living in a particular area and their environment. An ecosystem can be described as a pyramid, but more accurately as a food web. A species is a group of related individual organisms that have the same characteristics or qualities, and who can breed with each other but not members of other species. A population is all of the individuals of a given species in a specific area at a certain time. And a community is all of the populations in a specific area at a certain time. The place in which a species lives is called its habitat. This term can be used to refer to a very large area or small area, dependent on the context in which you are talking. Phytoplankton is the primary producers of the sea and forms the basis of the marine ecosystem. Primary carnivores eat primary producers; secondary carnivores eat primary carnivores and so forth. At each step 90 percent of the energy is lost. Some species benefit from other species without eating each other. We call these types of relationships symbiotic relationships. There are three types of symbiotic relationship: 1) a mutualism, where both organisms benefit from each other; 2) commensalism, where only one organism actually benefits from the relationship, but the other organism is not harmed; 3) parasitism, where one organism benefits from the relationship, and in doing so harms the other organism.

Find out more:

http://en.wikipedia.org/wiki/Benthic_zone
http://en.wikipedia.org/wiki/Pelagic_zone
http://en.wikipedia.org/wiki/Euphotic_zone
http://en.wikipedia.org/wiki/Aphotic_zone
http://en.wikipedia.org/wiki/Ecosystem
https://en.wikipedia.org/wiki/Marine_biology
http://en.wikipedia.org/wiki/Symbiosis

THE PHYSICS OF DIVING

Physics is about how the environment interacts with you. Water is denser than air, and this influences how heat, light and sound behave. After that, we have a look at pressure, and how pressure, volume, air consumption and temperature are related. We will talk about how different gases, such as oxygen and nitrogen, have their own pressure, that is, their partial pressure. We will turn to gasses in a fluid, how they saturate and super-saturate a fluid. Lastly, we will talk about calculating buoyancy. There are some calculations to do, but they are easy, more like using your common sense than anything else. Before we start, let's refresh your memory on atoms and molecules. Matter is made out of small particles: atoms or atoms glued together, molecules. In solid matter, they hardly move around. In a liquid they do move around, and in a gas they move around a lot. How quick they move, and with how energy the bump together is what we feel as temperature. If the temperature goes up, the speed of the atoms or molecules goes up, and they bump more violently into each other. That means they take up more space, and the density of the gas or liquid goes down: there are less atoms or molecules per litre.

By the way, atoms are really, really, really small. For instance, there are

78 000 000 000 000 000 000	atoms in a grain of sand
6 000 000 000	people on earth

Or, you can see how many there are also like this. Radium is a radioactive metal because its atoms fall apart by itself. In one gram of radium, every second, 136 000 000 000 atoms are destroyed and turned into radioactive energy. And this will go on for thousands of years in that one single gram of radium.

Ok, enough. Let's start.

Find out more:

This is an animation of moving atoms

More information about atoms

Heat

Conduction, Convection, Radiation.

Heat never stays in one place. We call this movement of heat 'heat transmission'. There are three different ways that heat moves (is transmitted): conduction, convection and radiation. For us divers, the most important of these is conduction. When the molecules of two bodies, for example your body and water, come into contact with each other, heat is transmitted, conducted from hot to cold, see Figure 14. When our warmer bodies come into contact with the cooler water our body heat is conducted to the water. This happens in air too, of course.

Conduction

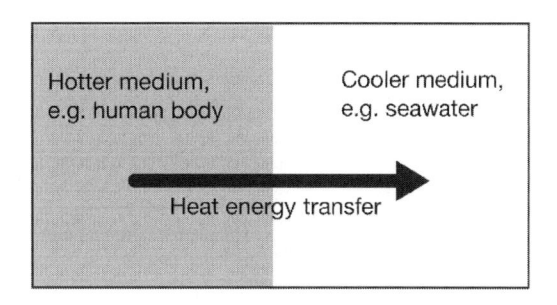

Hotter medium, e.g. human body

Cooler medium, e.g. seawater

Heat energy transfer

Convection

Cooler, denser water sinks and pushes less dense warmer water up and takes its place.

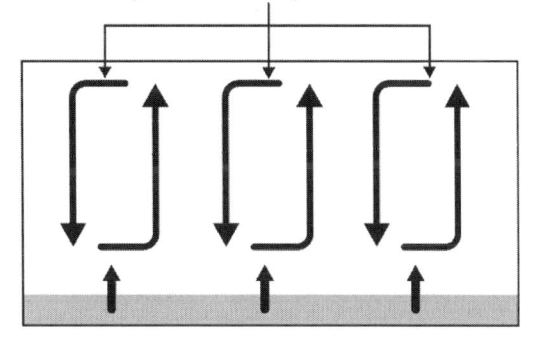

Radiation

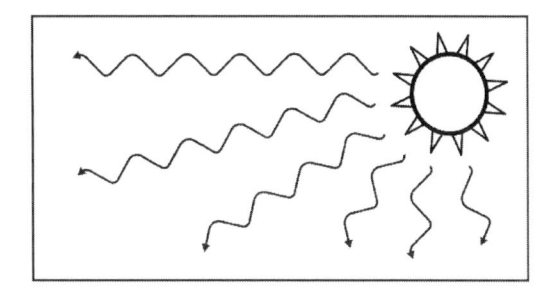

Heat energy is transferred by electromagnetic waves e.g. heat from the sun.

Figure 14 Heat Movement: Conduction, Convection and Radiation

But because the atoms of a liquid, such as water, are much closer together than the atoms in air, the heat from your body is transferred very quickly into the water. In fact, water conducts heat more than 20 times faster than air. On a sunny day of 25°C you would remain warm in a t-shirt, but if you are immersed in water of 25°C wearing the same t-shirt you would quickly become cold. This is the reason why we wear wetsuits (wetsuits are made of neoprene, which is contains tiny air bubbles that isolate our skin from the water) and dry-suits (dry-suits trap a layer of air between your body and the water) when diving. These form a barrier between our skin and the water that slows down conduction of heat between skin and water. Convection is the second form of heat transmission. Convection does affect us divers a bit, but not nearly as much as conduction. It works like this: when you are diving, your body heat is conducted into the water surrounding you, and so the water heats up. The water atoms of the warmer water move faster and collide harder with each other, pushing them further apart from each other. Because of this, the water becomes less dense, and it rises because cooler, denser water pushes it out of the way, up, and takes its place (this is how a hot air balloon works). The rising warmer water means that your skin is exposed to new, colder water. Your body heat is now transferred by conduction to these 'new' cold water atoms and they in turn rise, and the process repeats. You can see this in Figure 14. The third and last way how heat moves is radiation. This does not affect us as divers. Radiation is heat energy transferred by electromagnetic waves (radio waves, microwaves, x-rays, ultraviolet rays), as you can see in Figure 14. The heat you feel from the Sun is an example of radiation. You are not hot enough to radiate. Sorry.

Key things to remember:

The three ways in which heat energy is transferred are conduction, convection, radiation. Water conducts heat than twenty times faster than air. We lose body heat underwater mainly through conduction. This heat loss is speeded up by convection. Heat loss through radiation does not affect us.

Find out more:

http://en.wikipedia.org/wiki/Heat_transfer

LIGHT

Refraction, Absorption, Diffusion and visual reversion.

Because water is denser than air, it also influences light differently. We will have a look at refraction, diffusion, and absorption. You will have seen the effect of refraction if you have ever placed a pencil in a glass of water, and seen that the pencil looks larger under the water than above, and that the 'two halves' of the pencil seem to be disconnected from each other. This is because light gets bent when passing from one medium (air) to another (water). Light passing underwater from the water to the air in your mask bends in such a way that everything seems larger and closer to us: 33 percent larger and 25 percent closer. So when divers brag about that the big fish they saw, it may have been big but not as large as it they think! See Figure 15.

Refraction

Without refraction

With refraction

Actual Perceived

The path of light bends as it passes from the water to the air in your mask.

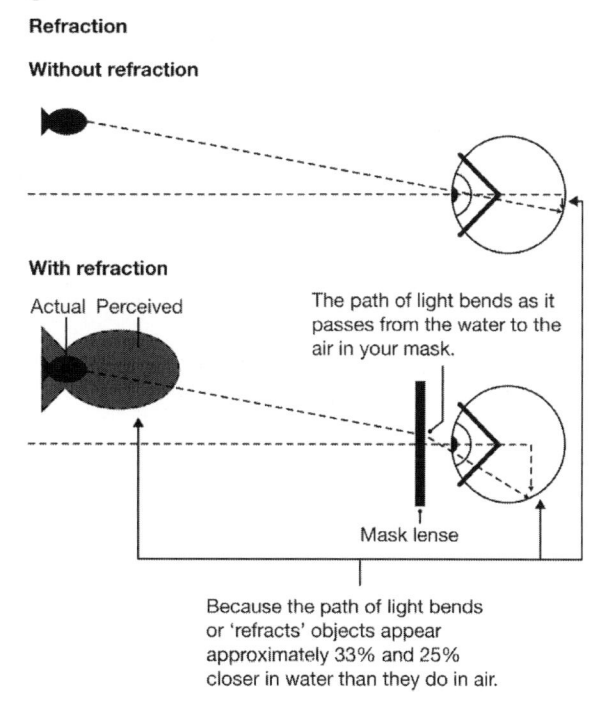

Mask lense

Because the path of light bends or 'refracts' objects appear approximately 33% and 25% closer in water than they do in air.

Figure 15 Refraction of light underwater

Under the best circumstances, you can look for about 80 meters under water, but you have to be extremely lucky to experience these perfect circumstances, and chances are you are not that lucky. You cannot see very far in water because light underwater gets spread out, diffused, by the water. This is diffusion: the way in which light is scattered underwater makes everything appear hazier, without sharp shadows. The effect of diffusion is much stronger if there are many suspended particles, currents or temperature differences.

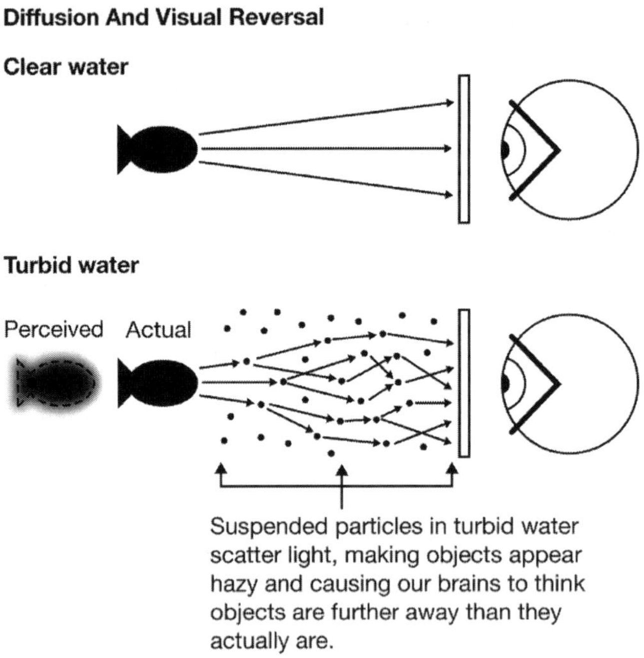

Diffusion And Visual Reversal

Clear water

Turbid water

Perceived   Actual

Suspended particles in turbid water scatter light, making objects appear hazy and causing our brains to think objects are further away than they actually are.

Figure 16 Turbidity and visual reversal

These cause the water to be turbid (cloudy). This makes everything appear particularly hazy and can cause an effect called visual reversal. Visual reversion is a strange thing, because unlike "normal" refraction, visual reversal causes things to appear further away than they are actually, instead of bigger and closer. See Figure 16. This is because is because the human brain evolved on land, where light travels through air and things usually only appear hazy and small if they are far away. Our brain makes the same assumption underwater: if something is hazy it must be far away. You may have noticed this if you have suddenly realised that you were closer to a wall then you thought when diving in low visibility.

Colour Absorption

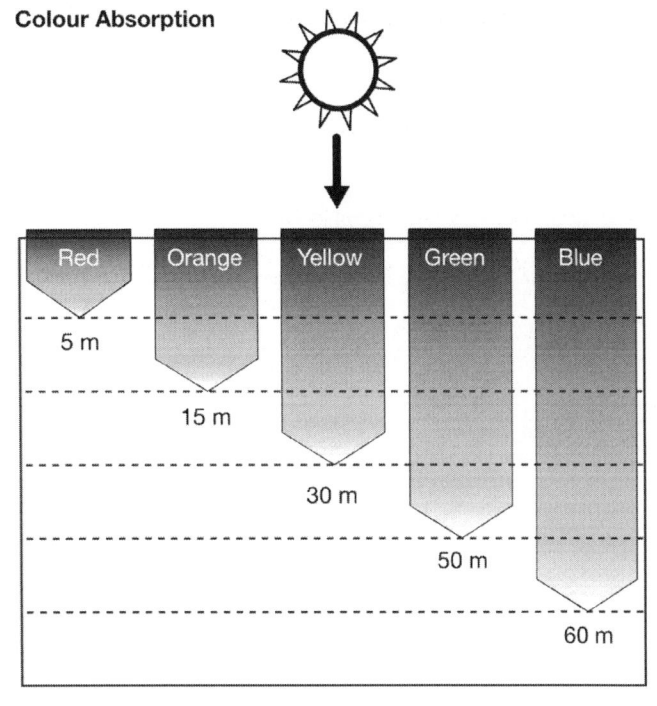

Figure 17 Absorption of light underwater

The third way how water affects light differently from air is by absorption. Water absorbs light, and the deeper you go, the more light is absorbed and the darker it gets. We can think of light as waves of energy that we can see. Waves of different wavelengths have different amounts of energy, and we see this as different colours (so, when you think about it, colour is just an illusion made in your brain. It does not exist, only wavelength exists.). Think of the rainbow. We see different bands of colour, but in reality there are no bands, just a continuous range of high to low wavelength. But anyway, the colour red comes first, it has the least energy and the longest wavelength (as with normal waves, a long wavelength means that few waves pass per second, and so not much energy is transported). As we progress through the rainbow, each colour has a more energy and a shorter wavelength. The colour blue comes last, and has the most energy and the shortest wavelength. Water absorbs colours with the least energy (so the longest wave lengths) more easily. This means that red light is the first to go, blue light is the last, as you can see in Figure 17. When you are on a deeper dive you will have noticed how blue everything looks. On a shallow reef you will see a lot more colour, but red will still appear to be a brown colour. You will notice absorption not only in a vertical direction, but also in a horizontal direction. The deeper you are and the further you are from something underwater, the fewer colours you will see. This is important to remember for underwater photography.

Key things to remember:

Refraction causes light to bend and makes everything underwater appear to be 33 percent larger and 25 percent closer than it is actually. Diffusion is the scattering of light. This happens more in turbid water and causes the effect of visual reversal, which makes things appear further away than they are really because they look hazy. Water absorbs light. It absorbs red first because it has the longest wavelength and the least energy and blue last because it has the shortest wavelength and the most energy.

Find out more:

http://en.wikipedia.org/wiki/Light

http://en.wikipedia.org/wiki/Underwater_vision

SOUND

Sound goes four times faster underwater,
Direction cannot be determined, but intensity can be determined.

Sound is a wave of atoms. The closer the atoms of a medium are together, the easier sound waves can travel.(Actually, it is not quite that simple, the elasticity of the bonds between the atoms is what matters, but usually that goes together with a high density). Water is denser than air, and the bonds between its atoms are very elastic, and that means that water conducts sound much better than air. The speed of sound under water is four times higher than it is in air. This creates a problem for us underwater. It means that we can hear sounds from farther away, but that we cannot tell from which direction the sound came from. This is because the human brain evolved to deal only with sounds travelling in air (we are land mammals, remember). Our brains estimate where a sound has come from by comparing the time that the sound arrived at one ear with the time it arrived at the other ear. Underwater sound travels too fast for our brain to be able to tell the difference, and therefore it sounds as if everything comes from above. Interestingly, animals on land with small heads, where the ears are close together have the same problem. They solve this by moving their heads, think of birds. Of course you can tell if a sound is getting louder or quieter as you swim, the sound intensity, and you can use that as a navigation aid to indicate whether you are swimming towards or away from the source of a sound, for example a boat engine.

Key things to remember:

Sound travels four times faster underwater than at the surface. You can hear sounds from farther away underwater, but you are unable to tell which direction a sound is coming from. You can however hear intensity changes (loud, soft) caused by the distance.

Find out more:

http://en.wikipedia.org/wiki/Underwater_acoustics

PRESSURE

The pressure of water: sea water: 1 bar per 10 meters, fresh water 1 bar per 10.3 meters. Ambient pressure and gauge pressure.

You probably know that because water is denser than air, water weighs more and puts more pressure on you than air does. At sea level, the air pushes with 1 Bar (atmosphere). If you dive into the sea, for every ten metres in seawater the pressure increases by 1 Bar (so that at 10 metres of seawater the pressure is 2 Bar, at 20 metres it is 3 Bar, at 30 metres it is 4 Bar and so forth). This is easy to remember: the pressure on any depth in the sea is 1 Bar of the air, plus 1 Bar for every ten meters you dive deeper. So to find out the pressure at your depth, you divide the depth by ten, and you add one (of the air).

Pressure = depth divided by 10, plus 1 = D/10 +1

Salt water is heavier than fresh water, because it has salt in it. Seawater has about 3% salt in it, and so it weighs 3% more. This means that every litre of seawater weighs 1.03 kilogram, whereas every litre of freshwater only weighs 1 kilogram. Less weight means less pressure: in fresh water you can go deeper (well, only 3%) that in salt water, and have the same pressure. Seawater is easier to calculate with than fresh water, because in seawater there is an increase of exactly 1 Bar of pressure every 10 metres, whereas in freshwater the pressure increases by 1 Bar every 10.3 metres.

We will soon be moving onto working out changes in the volume of a flexible container and changes in a diver's air consumption at different depths. To do that we need to be more accurate in working out the pressure at a given depth, rather than just being able to say that it is 2 Bar at 10 metres, 3 Bar at 20 metres etc. For example, we may need to be able to work out the pressure is at 23 metres of seawater or of freshwater. It is easy to do. Let's look at how.

Let's take 23 metres of seawater as an example first, because sea water is easiest. We know that there is 1 Bar of pressure at the surface, and 1 Bar of pressure for every 10 metres of water. First we will work out the pressure of the water and then add the 1 Bar of surface pressure. If seawater exerts 1 Bar of pressure every 10 metres, then we must take the depth – 23 metres – and divide it by 10 metres.

23 metres ÷ 10 metres = 2.3 Bar (Dividing by 10 is easy, just put a dot between the numbers!)

Now don't forget to add the 1 Bar of surface pressure.

2.3 Bar + 1 Bar = 3.3 Bar

Now let's work out the pressure at 23 metres of freshwater. Again work out the water pressure first, and then add the 1 Bar of surface pressure. (Don't forget to do that! It's a common mistake people make.) Remember that in freshwater there is 1 Bar of pressure every 10.3 metres, so instead of dividing the depth by 10 metres as we do in seawater, we divide it by 10.3 metres. You may want to use a calculator for this one.

23 metres ÷ 10.3 metres = 2.2330097087379 Bar

That number is a bit long! Let's round it to two decimal places. Then we have 2.23 Bar. Or we could make it even simpler and round to one decimal place. Then we have 2.2 Bar. (Remember when rounding, if the number after is less than 5 you keep the number the same, if it is 5 or more you round the number up. So, for instance, 9.42 becomes 9.4, but 9.48 becomes 9.5) Don't forget to add the 1 Bar of surface pressure.

2.2 Bar + 1 Bar = 3.2 Bar

So, to remember:

In salt water: Pressure = Depth divided by 10, plus one

In fresh water: Pressure = Depth divided by 10.3, plus one

AMBIENT PRESSURE, ABSOLUTE PRESSURE AND GAUGE PRESSURE

The word ambient means 'of the surrounding area or environment', so the ambient pressure means the pressure of the surrounding area. It is the pressure pushing on you when you are diving. The ambient pressure at 23 metres of seawater is 3.3 Bar, because the pressure of the surrounding environment includes the water pressure and the surface pressure. They also call this pressure the absolute pressure. Gauge pressure is something else. It is simply the pressure of the water only. So, you do not add the one Bar of the air, and that is the only difference. So, the gauge pressure at 23 metres of seawater is 2.3 Bar. We don't need to add the 1 Bar of surface pressure. You can also say it like this: gauge pressure is always 1 bar less than the absolute pressure. See Figure 18.

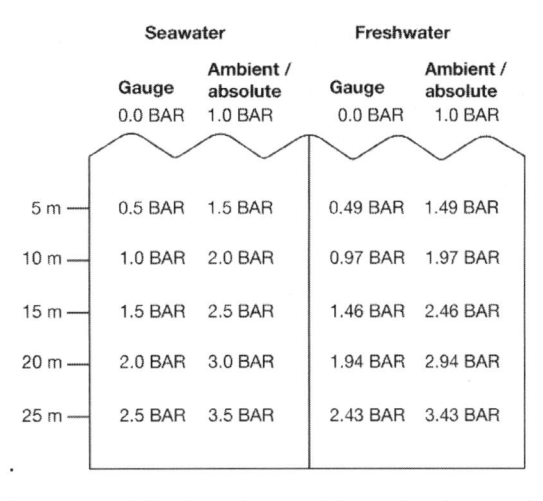

	Seawater		Freshwater	
	Gauge	Ambient / absolute	Gauge	Ambient / absolute
Surface	0.0 BAR	1.0 BAR	0.0 BAR	1.0 BAR
5 m	0.5 BAR	1.5 BAR	0.49 BAR	1.49 BAR
10 m	1.0 BAR	2.0 BAR	0.97 BAR	1.97 BAR
15 m	1.5 BAR	2.5 BAR	1.46 BAR	2.46 BAR
20 m	2.0 BAR	3.0 BAR	1.94 BAR	2.94 BAR
25 m	2.5 BAR	3.5 BAR	2.43 BAR	3.43 BAR

Figure 18 Pressure in salt water and fresh water, ambient, absolute and gauge pressure

Key things to remember:

Water is denser than air, and so it weighs more and exerts more pressure than air. Because seawater weighs more than freshwater, at a given depth there is more pressure in seawater than in fresh water. In seawater there is an increase of 1 Bar of pressure every 10 metres, whereas in freshwater the pressure increases by 1 Bar every 10.3 metres. Ambient and absolute pressure mean the same thing: the total pressure of the water and air pressure at the surface. Gauge pressure is only the water pressure: ambient pressure minus one Bar. You can calculate the gauge pressure by taking the depth and dividing this by 10 for salt water, or dividing by 10.3 for fresh water. If you add 1 bar to this, you have calculated the ambient pressure.

THE RELATIONSHIP OF PRESSURE TO THE VOLUME AND DENSITY OF A GAS (BOYLE'S LAW)

Boyle's law: If the pressure goes up, volume goes the same amount down.

What does pressure do to you? They good news is that it has no effect on the parts of you where there is no air (and that is biggest part of you). Unfortunately, it does compress the air spaces inside of you, for instance in your ears, or lungs. Pressure pushes the atoms of a gas, such as air, closer together. The same number of molecules occupy a smaller space. So, under pressure, the volume of the gas becomes smaller but the density becomes greater. It can help to imagine taking a balloon underwater. As you take it down and the pressure increases, the balloon gets smaller, but it has the same number of air molecule in it – the air cannot escape. The volume goes down, and so the density must go up. Now, when you take your balloon up again, and the pressure decreases, it gets bigger again: the volume increases, and density decreases.

Look at it this way: if the pressure goes up, the volume goes down. If the volume goes down, the density goes up. The nice thing is that Mr Boyle discovered a few hundreds of years ago that these changes always happen in the same way. If you make the pressure four times as high, the volume becomes four times as small, and the density becomes four times as big. Or if you make the pressure ten times as high, the volume becomes ten times as small, and the density becomes ten times as big. If you know the change in pressure, you know it all! Boyle got his name in history with this simple discovery, and we are going use his law to calculate changes in volume.

Calculating Volume

Calculate volume and density by multiplying or dividing with the ambient pressure.

Just as we talk about weight in kilograms, we talk about volume in litres. Now, imagine taking that balloon underwater. Let's say that the balloon has a volume of 6 litres at the surface, and we take the balloon to 20 metres of seawater. At 20 metres of seawater the pressure is 3 Bar: 3 times more pressure than at the surface (if you cannot calculate this yourself, go back to the section about pressure underwater). The pressure is three times greater, so the volume of the balloon is three times smaller, therefore we must divide the volume of the balloon by three. Remember this: you can only make things smaller by dividing them, multiplying makes them bigger. (More means Multiply, Less mean Divide!)

6 litres ÷ 3 Bar = 2 litre

So, at 30 meters in the sea, the balloon with a volume of six litres now is three times smaller, so it only is two litres, see Figure 19. That is a bit of an easy sum, let's try one that is a bit more difficult. Let's take difficult numbers and fresh water! Imagine the balloon has a volume of 14 litres at the surface, and we take it down to 32 metres of fresh water. First, we need to know the pressure at 32 metres of freshwater. It is depth divided by 10.3 (not 10, remember, fresh water!), plus one, so 32 divided by 10.3 plus 1 and that is 4.1 Bar. There is 4.1 times more pressure than at the surface. The pressure is 4.1 times greater, so the volume of the balloon will be 4.1 times smaller, therefore we must divide the volume of the balloon by 4.1. See Figure 19. 14 litres ÷ 4.1 Bar = 3.41 litres (rounded to 2 decimal places)

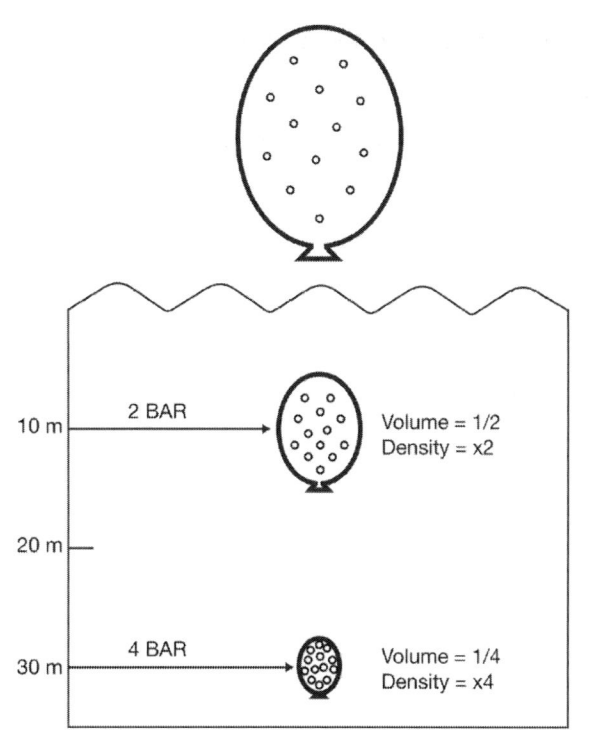

Figure 19 A balloon at different depth, changes of volume and density

Now we take one step further: you can also take a balloon from one depth to another depth and calculate the volume. You can even can take a balloon from a certain depth in sea water to another depth in fresh water and calculate the volume! The trick is to always begin with bringing your balloon back up to surface, and calculate the volume of your balloon at the surface.

A balloon has volume of 10 litres at 17 metres of sea water. What is the new volume at 28 meters? Trick: bring it up to the surface. That means the balloon gets bigger, and More Means Multiply. Multiply by the pressure, of course.

At 17 metres seawater the pressure is 17÷10 +1 = 2.7 Bar

At the surface it is only 1 Bar

So the balloon becomes 2.7 times bigger: 10 litres x 2.7 = 27 litres.

Now we can go with our balloon back into the sea to a new depth, or in fresh water to a new depth: Shall we go to 28 meters of seawater? The balloon will become smaller, so we have to divide.

The pressure there is 28÷10 plus 1 = 3.8 Bar.

Our balloon of 27 litres becomes 3.8 times smaller: 27 ÷ 3.8 = 7.11 litres.

Or we go to freshwater, say 15 metres deep. Our balloon will also become smaller here, of course, so again we divide.

The pressure here is 15÷10.3 (remember, not 10, it is fresh water!) plus 1 = 2.4 Bar.

Our balloon becomes 2.4 times smaller, so 27÷2.4 = 11.3 litres.

So, don't be scared if you get a question like: a balloon with a volume of 11.2 litres at 23.6 metres of sea water is taken to 11.5 metres of fresh water. What is the new volume? Just take your balloon back to the surface, calculate the volume there, and bring it back down. That is all. If it helps, you may want to draw your working out as a diagram like Figure 20:

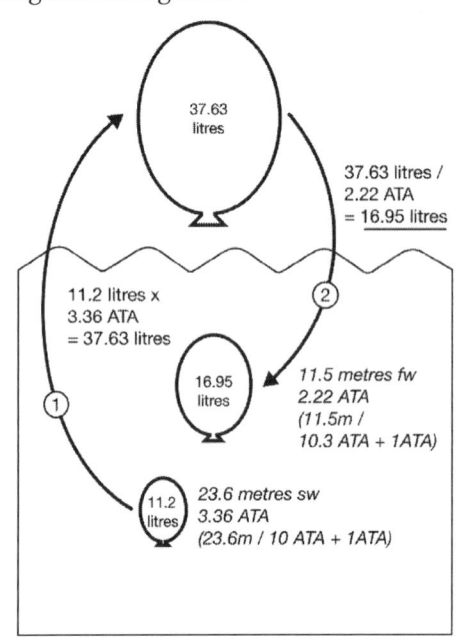

Figure 20 Bringing a balloon up and down to calculate the volume

WARNING. IF YOU DO NOT LIKE FORMULAS AND ALGEBRA, DO NOT READ THIS!!!

Alternatively, if you prefer to work with equations, the equation (where V_1 is original volume, V_2 is the new volume and P_1 is original pressure and P_2 is new pressure) looks like this:

$V_2 = (V_1 \times P_1) \div P_2$

CALCULATING AIR CONSUMPTION

Calculate air consumption by multiplying or dividing with the ambient pressure.

Why are we bringing balloons up and down? Because this is the way you can calculate your air consumption at different depths! We all know that we use more air on a deeper dive than on a shallower dive. Let's start simple. Let's say that we already know how much air a diver uses per minute at the surface. Let's keep it really simple and say that he uses 2 Bar of air per minute. How many Bar of air would he use per minute at 25 metres of seawater? We know for a start that he will use more than 2 Bar a minute, not less, and more is multiplication. First we need to know what the pressure is at 25 metres of seawater, which is

25 10 +1 = 3.5 Bar.

Because the pressure is 3.5 times more, he will be using 3.5 times as much air as at the surface. So all we have to do is multiply 2 Bar per minute by 3.5 Bar.

2 Bar per minute x 3.5 Bar = 7 Bar per minute

Let us take the last step, and calculate how much air a diver uses at different depths.

A diver uses 5 Bar per minute on 15 meters? How much does this diver use at 22 meters. The diver is in salt water. Here we go. The trick was to bring the diver to the surface. What is the pressure at 15 meters of sea water?

15÷10 +1 = 2.5

You know a diver uses less at the surface, so less is dividing:

5÷2.5 = 2 Bar per minute.

Now we can go to the new depth. First find out what the pressure is there:

22÷10 + 1 = 3.2.

You know that a diver uses more air at depth, and more is multiplying:

2 Bar at surface x 3.2 = 6.4 Bar per minute.

And that is it. One last remark: Volume and density can only change with pressure in flexible containers. You tank is not flexible, so nothing changes inside your tank if you do not breath and empty it. The pressure, volume and density of a closed tank are always same, no matter how high the pressure around the tank is!

Key things to remember:

If the pressure goes up, the volume goes the same amount down, and the density goes up by the same amount. This is called Boyle's Law. To work out the new volume of a balloon when taking it from the surface to a specific depth, divide the original volume by the pressure at the depth to which you are descending. To work out the new volume of a balloon when taking it from a specific depth to the surface, multiply the original volume by the pressure at the depth from which you are going up. To work out how much air a diver will breathe per minute at a given depth, bring him to the surface, multiply this surface air consumption rate (Bar per min) by the pressure at the new depth

Partial Pressure (Dalton's Law)

Air consists of 79% Nitrogen and 21% Oxygen.
At one Bar, the partial pressure of Nitrogen is 0.79 bar,
At one Bar, the partial pressure of Oxygen 0.21 Bar:

We have talked about the pressure at the surface (at sea level) being 1 Bar. Air is made up mainly from two different gases: oxygen and nitrogen (there are small amounts of other gases but we don't need to talk about them). 21 percent of air is oxygen and 79 percent is nitrogen. So 21 percent of the pressure comes from oxygen, and 79 percent of the pressure comes from nitrogen. We call the pressure each gas exerts the Partial Pressure (PP), because it is part of the total. We can say: in air at 1 Bar, the partial pressure PP of Nitrogen is 0.79 Bar and the PP Oxygen is 0.21 Bar. (And this how Mr Dalton got his name in history in 1801, too easy really.)

When we descend on a dive to 10 metres, the total pressure of the air we are breathing increases to 2 Bar, double what it was at the surface. The partial pressure of each gas will also be double what it was at the surface. To work out the partial pressure of each gas we simply multiply the surface partial pressure by the new pressure, in this case two:

0.79 PP N_2 x 2 = 1.58 PP N_2

0.21 PP O_2 x 2 = 0.42 PP O_2

To check, they should be 2 Bar together:

1.58 PP N_2 + 0.42 PP O_2 = 2 Bar

The percentage of the gases in your tank has not changed of course! Nitrogen still makes up 79 percent of this pressure and oxygen 21 percent of the air. Only the PP at what you breathe the air from your tank has changed at depth. You can see all this in Figure 21.

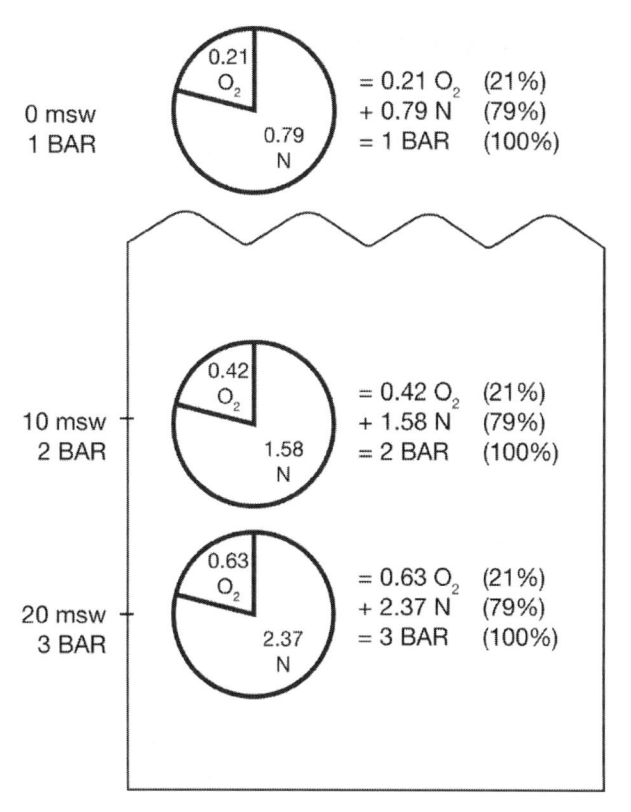

Figure 21 Partial Pressure and depth

Some gases can become dangerous when they reach certain (partial) pressure. That includes oxygen! We need oxygen to live, but like anything, too much of a good thing is bad. We will talk more about the effects of oxygen toxicity in the physiology of diving, but let's talk now about the pressure at which it can become toxic. Oxygen can become toxic to humans when it reaches a pressure of 1.4 Bar. With a tank filled with normal air, how deep can we go before we hit this limit? We get there when 1.4 Bar is 0,21 of the total pressure, so the total pressure must be:

1.4 ÷ 0.21 (PP O$_2$) = 6.6 Bar.

When is the total pressure 6.6 Bar? We take the one Bar from the air away, and there is 5.6 Bar left. With 1 Bar per 10 m, that means 56 meters.

Now, let's work out what the partial pressure of oxygen in normal air is at the recreational diving depth limit of 40 metres:

0.21 PP O$_2$ x 5 Bar = 1.05 PP O$_2$

So you are quite safe.

Because nitrogen limits our dive time, we can use a blend of gas that has less nitrogen and more oxygen to extend our dive time: Enriched Air (Nitrox). However, because the percentage of oxygen is higher, oxygen can now become a concern within recreational limits. For example we could use a blend of gas that has 66 percent nitrogen and 34 percent oxygen. In this blend the nitrogen has a partial pressure of 0.66 PP N₂ and the oxygen 0.34 PP O₂. If we dive with this blend at 25 metres of seawater let's see what the partial pressure of the oxygen would be:

0.34 PP O₂ x 3.5 Bar = 1.19 PP O₂

This is still well within the limit but you can see that we are getting closer. Now let's see what happens at 32 metres:

0.34 PP O₂ x 4.2 Bar = 1.42 PP O₂

We are now over the limit. When you dive with Nitrox you always need to check what your maximum depth is for your particular blend of Nitrox.

The other gas that could be a concern to us is carbon monoxide. Carbon monoxide is never good, and it should never be in your tank, but let's suppose that there is a small amount in the air that you are breathing. At the surface this small amount may not be very harmful to you (smokers are always taking in small amounts of carbon monoxide!) but when you breathe it under pressure during a dive it does quickly becomes harmful. Let's say that 0.5 percent of the air you are breathing is carbon monoxide. At 30 metres, at 4 Bar, this will have increased to 4 x 0.5% = 2 % CO. So now the air you are breathing has the equivalent of 2 percent of CO, four times as much. This is sometimes called 'equivalent percentages': how much you would have to breathe on the surface to get the same effect. Here that is four times as much, so breathing 0.5% CO at 30 metres is equivalent to breathing four times as much on surface: the equivalent percentage on the surface is 2% CO. Understand this: the actual percentage in your tank does not change of course, it is just a way of looking at it.

Key things to remember:

The partial pressure of a gas is the percentage of the pressure caused by that specific gas in a mix of gases. It is the percentage of the gas in the mix multiplied with the pressure of the mix. 21 percent of air is oxygen and 79 percent is nitrogen. At sea level the total pressure of air is 1 Bar. The partial pressure of nitrogen is 0.79 Bar (PP N₂) and the partial pressure of oxygen is 0.21 Bar (PP O₂). Oxygen can become toxic at 56 metres when breathing normal air, but at shallower depths when breathing enriched air Nitrox. Also, carbon monoxide is very dangerous under high partial pressure.

THE RELATIONSHIP OF TEMPERATURE PRESSURE AND VOLUME (CHARLES' LAW)

If the temperature goes up or down and the volume cannot change, pressure goes up or down with 0.6 bar per degree Celsius (Charles' law).

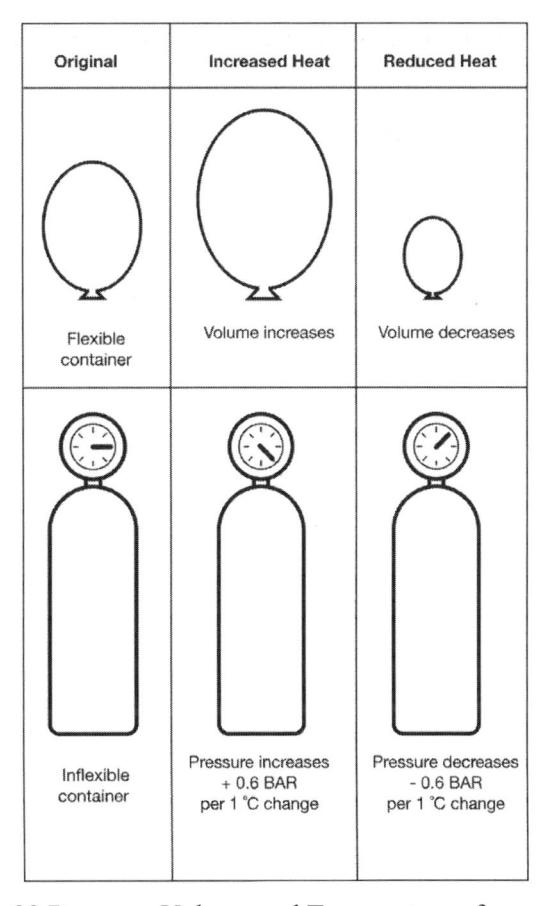

Figure 22 Pressure, Volume and Temperature of a gas

When a gas gets hotter, its atoms begin to move faster and collide more. If the container that contains the gas is flexible, like a balloon, the atoms will take up more space as they move faster. If it is not flexible, like your tank, they cannot take up more space, and so the pressure increases. The opposite will happen if the gas becomes cooler, the atoms will move around less and they will take up less space or cause less pressure. The changes in pressure are most interesting to us. When we heat the gas your tank, the pressure will go up by 0.6 Bar per 1°C of temperature change. And of course, if you cool your tank, the pressure drops by 0.6 Bar per 1°C of temperature change. See Figure 22.

Let us have a look how that works out on a dive. You have a tank filled to 200 Bar at 25°C (you are diving somewhere nice and sunny, of course), and then go diving in water of 10°C (you made a mistake, not that nice), you can work out much pressure you will have lost from your tank:

25°C - 10°C = 15°C change in temperature

15°C x 0.6 Bar = 9 Bar

So you will have used 9 Bar of air before you even begin the dive! We sometimes fill scuba tanks in buckets of cool water, because the filling process creates heat, which temporarily increases the air pressure in the tank before it cools off. If we don't use cool water buckets, we take this heat increase into account and overfill the tank slightly.

Key things to remember:

When we heat the gas in a flexible container the volume will go up, and the volume will decrease as the gas cools down. When we heat the gas in an inflexible container the pressure will go up, and pressure will go down as the gas cools. For every 1°C temperature change, the pressure will increase or decrease by 0.6 Bar.

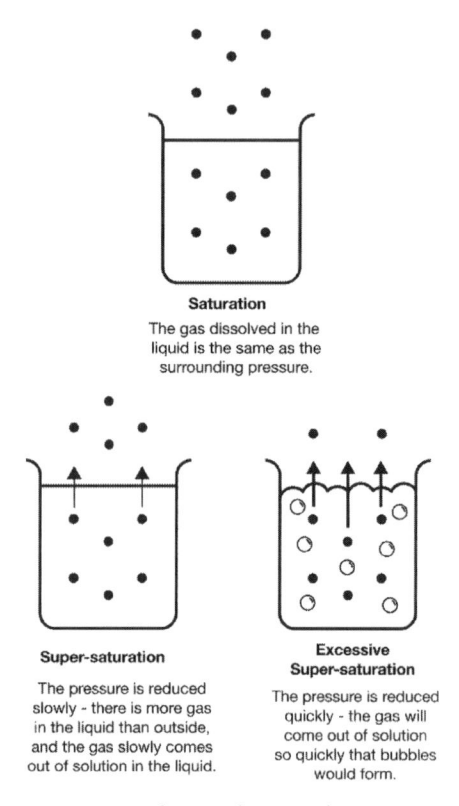

SATURATION, SUPER-SATURATION AND EXCESSIVE SUPER-SATURATION

Saturation, Super saturation, Excessive Super saturation and bubble formation.

Saturation
The gas dissolved in the liquid is the same as the surrounding pressure.

Super-saturation
The pressure is reduced slowly - there is more gas in the liquid than outside, and the gas slowly comes out of solution in the liquid.

Excessive Super-saturation
The pressure is reduced quickly - the gas will come out of solution so quickly that bubbles would form.

Figure 23 Saturation, super saturation and excessive super saturation

You cannot see it happen, but a gas enters a liquid easily. Oxygen and nitrogen particles go in and out a glass of water at the table, for instance. But how much goes in and out? Gas dissolves into a liquid until the pressure of the gas in the liquid is the same as the pressure on the outside liquid. So in our glass, the pressure of both of these gases dissolved in the water is 1 Bar, the same as the surrounding air pressure. Of that Bar, 0.21 Bar is oxygen and 0.79 Bar is nitrogen. That is exactly the pressure of oxygen and nitrogen in the glass as well. If we were to increase the surrounding pressure to 2 Bar by putting the glass of water into recompression chamber, more gas would dissolve into the water until the pressure of the gas in solution in the liquid also was 2 Bar, in the same oxygen and nitrogen percentages. We call this saturation: in a saturated liquid: the pressure inside and outside are equal.

What would happen now if we reduced the pressure again? The liquid can no longer hold that much gas and it must come out of solution. If we reduce the pressure slowly, there is more gas in the liquid than outside. This is called super-saturation. If we quickly reduce the pressure, the gas will come out of solution so quick that bubbles would form. This is called a state of excessive super-saturation.

Excessive super-saturation is what happens when you open a bottle of coke. Before you open the bottle, the pressure of the gas in the air space in the bottle is the same as the pressure of the gas dissolved in the coke. When you open the bottle you quickly reduce the air pressure and bubbles form in the coke. It is also what happens when a diver gets decompression sickness. Our bodies are mainly made up of water. At the surface our blood and tissues have the same amount of nitrogen dissolved in them as the surrounding pressure. When we descend underwater and the pressure increases, more nitrogen dissolves into solution in our bodies. As we go up and the pressure decreases, it comes out of solution again. As long as we go up slowly and therefore decrease the pressure slowly, the nitrogen comes out of solution slowly and no bubbles form. Our bodies are in a state of super-saturation. If, however, we go up too quickly, and reduce the pressure too quickly, too much nitrogen tries to come out of solution at one time and bubbles form. Our bodies would be in a state of excessive super-saturation. We will talk more about this in the section on decompression theory.

Key things to remember:

In a saturated liquid, the pressure of the gas dissolved in the liquid is the same as the pressure of the gas in contact with the liquid. In a supersaturated liquid, the pressure of the gas dissolved in the liquid is less than pressure of the gas in contact with the liquid. But the difference in pressure is not too big, and the gas slowly comes out of solution without forming bubbles. In an excessively supersaturated liquid, the pressure of the gas dissolved in the liquid is less than pressure of the gas in contact with the liquid. The difference in pressure is so great that the gas comes out of solution too quickly and forms bubbles.

BUOYANCY

Buoyancy and the weight of displaced water.
Positive, neutral, and negative buoyancy.

Let step into a bath, filled to the rim with nice hot water. As you step into it, it overflows. Your body pushes the water away. Your body displaces exactly the same volume of water as it needs to get into the bath. Suppose we collect that displaced water, and we weigh it. Do we know anything interesting now? Yes we do. The weight of that water is strength of the force that pushes you upwards in your bath. The water wants to be in the space where your body is, but it cannot, because, well, your body is lying there. So it starts pushing you up. It wants you out, it wants to get the space that you take in back.

You can see it like this: there are two forces working on your body in your bath. Pulling you down is, as usual, gravity, equal to your weight. Pushing you up is the water that wants to take the place of your body. If you know how much water your body displaces, so the volume of the water you displace, you can easily calculate how much that water weighs. And that is exactly the force pushing you up. Whether you float or sink depends on which of these two forces is stronger.

If the weight of the object is more than the weight of the water it displaces, gravity will win and the object will sink. An example of this is a coin that sinks: a coin may not weigh very much, but it does not displace much water either. Its volume is so small that the weight of the water it displaces is even less than the weight of the penny. It sinks. We call this negative buoyancy.

If the weight of the object is less than the weight of the water it displaces, the force of the water 'pushing' (buoying) the object up wins, and the object will float. An example of this is the ocean liner that floats: it may weigh a lot, but it also displaces a lot of water. The weight of that water is even higher than the weight of the ship. It floats. We call this positive buoyancy. If the weight of the object is exactly the same as the weight of the water it displaces, then both forces are equal and the object will be suspended in the water, it will neither float nor sink. This, of course, is the state we aim for when we are diving, and we call it neutral buoyancy.

So it is all about that weight of the object and the weight of the water that is displaced. This is interesting, because a litre of sea water weighs more than a litre of fresh water! (you have seen this already during your pressure calculations). Fresh water weighs 1 kilo per litre, so that makes it very easy to calculate (long live the metric system!). Salt water weighs 3% more, because there is 3% salt in it. Sea water weighs 1.03 kg per litre. This means salt water pushes you up more than fresh water. You float more easily in salt water. The saltier it is, the easier you float.

CALCULATING BUOYANCY

Weight pulls an object down, and buoyancy pushes it up.
Buoyancy equals the volume of the displaced water divided by the weight of the water per litre.
Fresh water: 1 litre weighs 1 kg, Sea water, 1 litre weighs 1.03 kg.

We can work out the buoyancy of an object (by how much it floats or sinks) if we know three things: how much the object weighs, the volume of the water the object displaces, and the weight of the water per litre. The last one is always the same: remember that seawater weighs 1.03 kg per litre and freshwater weighs 1 kg per litre.

Let's start off with an object in fresh water that weighs 50 kg and displaces 40 litres of water. First of all, write that out clearly.

Object weight: 50 kg

Volume of water the object displaces: 40 litres

Weight per litre of fresh water: 1 kg

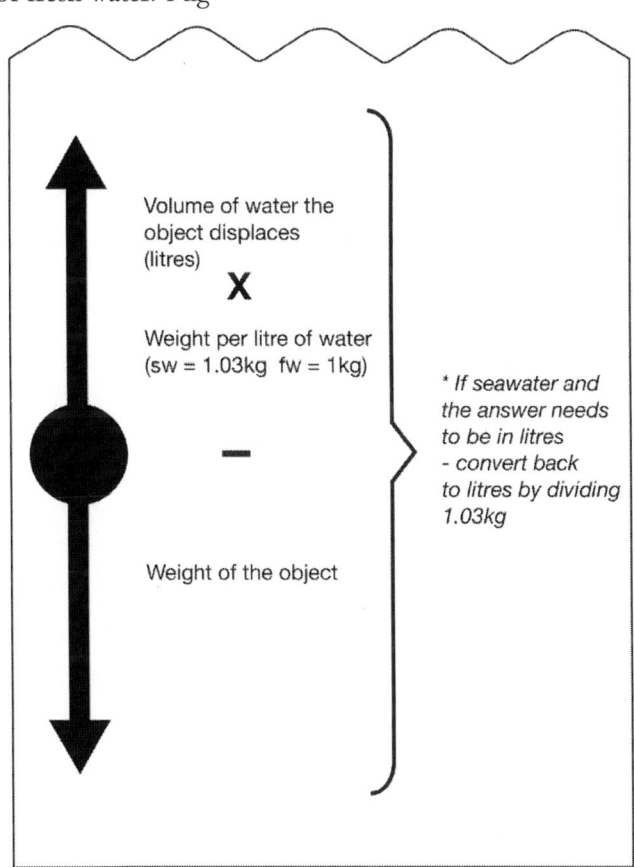

Figure 24 Buoyancy sum diagram

We strongly advise strongly to always make a drawing like Figure 24 when you are solving questions like this. They help you to think, and see it in your mind.

You want to find out how much 40 litres of fresh water weighs. Each of those 40 litres weighs 1KG, so we need to multiply 40 litres by 1 kg.

40 litres x 1 kg = 40 kg

51

Now you can work out the difference between the weight of the object and the weight of the water it displaces, and this is how negatively buoyant the object is. To do this, subtract the smaller number from the larger number.

50 kg (going down) – 40 kg (Going up) = 10 kg (going down).

You can use arrows instead of writing going up or going down of course! So, our object is 10 kg negatively buoyant. It lies on the bottom, and gravity is still pulling it down with 10 kg. Suppose I want to bring it up with a lift bag. I can work out exactly how much air I need to add to it to make it neutrally buoyant. Remember that neutrally buoyant means the force up is just as strong as the force down. I need to get the water push exactly 10 kg more. But how many litres of fresh water is exactly 10 kg? How much is the volume I have to displace with my lift bag? 10 litres of course, because 10 divided by one is ten.

So in fresh water it is really simple. In salt water you do exactly the same, it just looks a bit more complicated because you have to multiply and divide by 1.03. You need a calculator. I will do the same sum again, but now in sea water, so you can see the difference.

Object weight: 50 kg

Volume of water the object displaces: 40 litres

Weight per litre of freshwater: 1.03 kg (so this is different!)

That means that this is different too: how much do 40 litres of sea water weigh? More than 40 kilos!

40 litres x 1.03 kg = 41.2 kg

We subtract this from the weight

50 kg – 41.2 kg = 8. 8 kg.

So that is correct. It is less negatively buoyant in salt water (remember in fresh water this was 10kg).

Now I only need 8.8 kg of sea water. That is again less than 8.8 litres, because sea water is heavier! Do not forget this last step, you have to divide again by 1.03, not just 1.

8.8 ÷ 1.03 = 8.5

I need 1.5 litres less sea water than fresh water!

Let's take a quick look at calculating the buoyancy of a positively buoyant object. We need the same information and use the same sums. Let's say that an object in seawater weighs 50 kg and displaces 80 litres of sea water.

Object weight: 50 kg

Volume of water the object displaces: 80 litres

Weight per litre of seawater: 1.03 kg

First work out how much 80 litres of seawater weighs.

80 litres x 1.03 kg = 82.4 kg

Now work out the difference between the weight of the object and the weight of the water it displaces.

82.4 kg – 50 kg = 32.4 kg

So the object is 32.4 kg positively buoyant. If I want to make the object neutrally buoyant I would need to add 32.4 kg of weight to it. If I wanted to make it sink I would need to add more weight. For example, if I wanted to make the object 20 kg negatively buoyant, I would need add 32.4 kg to make it neutrally buoyant, and another 20 kg to make it 20 kg negatively buoyant.

32. Kg + 20 kg = 52 kg.

It is important to note that you must know the weight of the object, the volume of the water it displaces and the weight per litre of the water, to be able to work out its buoyancy. If you are missing any of these three pieces of information you cannot work it out. For example if an object is positively buoyant in seawater and weighs 50 kg, you cannot work out how much weight to add to make it neutrally buoyant, because you don't know how much water it displaces and therefore by how much it positively buoyant. However, if an object is neutrally buoyant and you know how much the object weighs, you can work out how much water it displaces. This is because the weight of the water it displaces must be the same as the weight of the object. For example if an object weighing 50 kg is neutrally buoyant in seawater, it must displace 50 kg of water, so you just need to work out how many litres is 50 kg of seawater.

50 kg ÷ 1.03 kg = 48.5 litres.

Key things to remember:

If the weight of the object is more than the weight of the water it displaces, the object will sink. We call this negative buoyancy. If the weight of the object is less than the weight of the water it displaces, the object will float. We call this positive buoyancy. If the weight of the object is the same as the weight of the water it displaces, the object will neither float nor sink. We call this neutral buoyancy. Because of the salt particles dissolved in seawater, it is heavier than freshwater. Seawater has more force with which to push or buoy an object up; objects are more buoyant in saltwater than in freshwater. We can work out the buoyancy of an object (by how much it floats or sinks) if we know three things: how much the object weighs, the volume of the water the object displaces, and the weight per litre of the water (the constant). Seawater weighs 1.03 kg per litre and freshwater weighs 1 kg per litre. To work out the buoyancy of an object, first find out the weight of the water the object displaces. Then find out the difference between the weight of the object and the weight of the water it displaces. If the object is positively buoyant, the difference in weight is how much weight you would need to add to the object to make it neutrally buoyant. Or if the object is negatively buoyant, you can then see how many litres of air you would need to add to a lift bag to make it neutrally buoyant, by dividing the difference in weight by the weight per litre of the water, either fresh water (1 kilogram per litre) or sea water (1.03 kilogram per litre).

DIVE EQUIPMENT

As a dive professional, you should be an expert about diving equipment and how it works. We cannot possibly begin to tell you about all the gear that is on the market. In fact, this is a very short chapter, because we will only explain the principles of the way your gear works. You will understand about steel tanks, aluminium tanks and the marks on them. We will talk about balanced and unbalanced regulators, and the different kinds of depth gauges.

TANKS

Steel and aluminium tanks. Burst disks.
Visual inspections and hydrostatic tests.
K-valves, DIN valves, and J valves.
Tank markings.

Steel Tank — Same internal capacity — **Aluminium Tank**

Lighter out of the water than aluminium tanks

Higher working pressure than aluminium tanks

More buoyant in the water than steel tanks

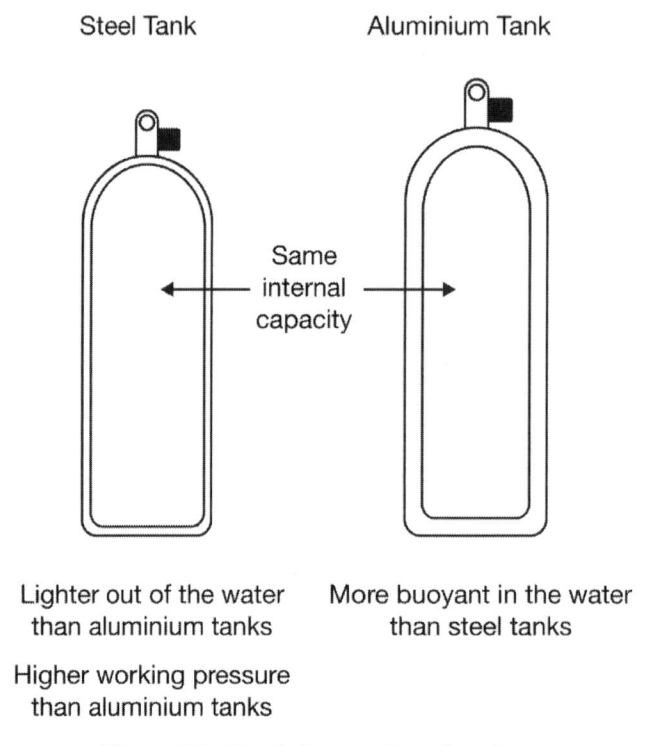

Figure 25 Aluminium and steel tanks

Tanks are made of either aluminium or steel. Steel is a stronger material, and that means that steel tanks can have more pressure with thinner walls. So, steel tanks are smaller and lighter out compared with aluminium tanks of the same internal capacity while the operational pressure (working pressure) of steel is higher than that of aluminium. Because steel tanks are smaller they displace less water, and so they are less buoyant. In fact, aluminium tanks become positively buoyant as they empty, but steel tanks just become a bit less negatively buoyant. You sink more easily with steel tanks, and need fewer weights. That is one of the reasons why steel tanks are widely used in cold water (diving in cold water requires a thick wetsuit or dry-suit and because these are very buoyant you need many weights, but if you have a steel tank you can do with less weights). Aluminium tanks are much more widely used in the humidity of the tropics, and it is not only because aluminium tanks are more buoyant. Another reason is that moisture (of which there is a lot in the tropics!) causes rust and when steel rusts it becomes weaker, whereas when aluminium rusts a protective layer is created that stops further rusting. See Figure 25.

Usually tanks have a safety valve, called a burst disk, which will burst when the pressure in the tank gets too high - higher than about 40% above the working pressure (or to put it another way, at 140% of the operating pressure). This is usually due to warming of the tank, for example, by the Sun. Such a valve is usually a simple piece of copper that breaks at a certain pressure. More expensive tanks have a burst disk on both sides of the tank, so that the tank does not start spinning if a valve bursts.

At least once a year, the inside and outside of the tank must be inspected for rust, dirt and damage: a visual inspection. This is also an opportunity to lubricate or replace the O-rings between the tank and the valve. This is important, because the tank and the valve are made of different metals, and when two metals come in contact they cause a weak electrical current. This is called galvanic action, and this causes rust, but rubber isolates and stops this. After a visual inspection, the inspector will place a sticker on the tank, with the date and their name, usually at the bottom of the tank.

An annual visual inspection is not enough. Once every three to seven years, depending on legal requirements a hydrostatic test needs to be done. A tester fills the tank with water (that is why it is called hydrostatic), and places the tank filled with water in a vat of water. The tank is pressurised typically around 60% higher than the working pressure (or in other words, 160% of the operational pressure). The tank expands because of the pressure and pushes the water out of the tank. How much water it displaces is dependent on how much the tank expands. If the tank expands too much, the tank walls were too weak, and the tank is rejected. The tester drills holes in the tank, or destroys the thread of the valve, so you cannot use it anymore. However, if all is well and your tank does not expand too much under high pressure, the tester gives the tank a stamp, and you can go diving with it again. A hydrostatic test is very important for safety, and you need to do one if you expect the tank was damaged by being dropping or if it has been exposed to temperatures above 82 degrees Celsius, which happens in a fire. You cannot take risks with metal under high pressure!

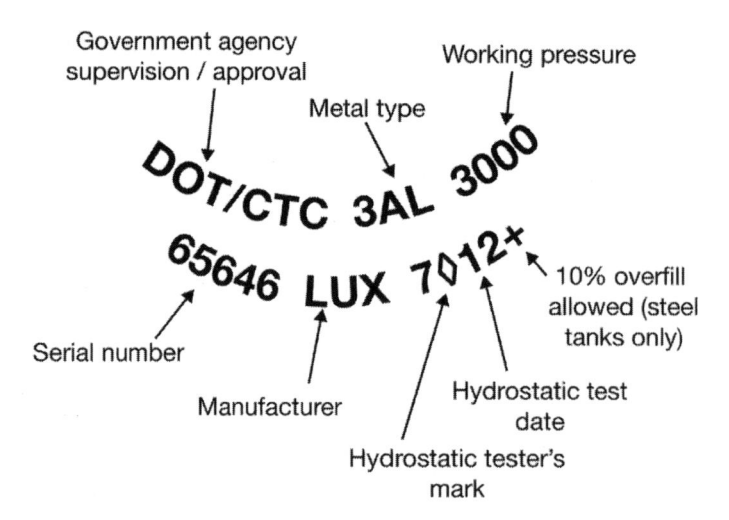

Diagram labels:
- Government agency supervision / approval → DOT/CTC
- Metal type → 3AL
- Working pressure → 3000
- Serial number → 65646
- Manufacturer → LUX
- Hydrostatic tester's mark → 7
- Hydrostatic test date → 12
- 10% overfill allowed (steel tanks only) → +

Figure 26 Markings on a tank

Let's look at the stamps on a tank in Figure 26.

DOT / CTC this is the **regulatory authority marking, the agency that tested the tank.**

3AL the metal. 3AL is aluminium, steel is 3AA

3000 The working pressure in psi (pressure per square inch)

65646 the unique serial number of your tank

LUX The manufacturer

7 12 + The stamp of the date of the latest hydrostatic test, the **+** means that the tank was strong enough to fill it with 10 percent more pressure than the normal operating pressure.

Your tank has a valve. There are two types of valves, a K-valve/yoke valve system, where the first stage of your regulator is clamped over the tank, and a DIN valve (*Deutsche Industrie Norme*) valve, where you screw the first stage into the tank. The DIN valve is stronger, and is usually used at higher operating pressures, technical diving or in overhead environments such as cave diving and wreck diving. Sometimes you may still see a J-valve. See Figure 27. A J-valve is an old system to let you know that your air is low (useful before we had SPGs). There's an extra spring that closes when the pressure has dropped to 50 Bar. You can then open that spring by pulling on a rope attached to it, and you can use the remaining 50 Bar to go up. That "pull down" gesture is what we still use to indicate that we are low on air.

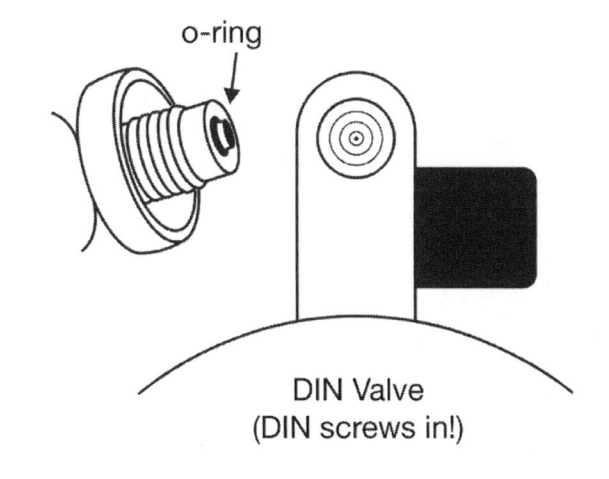

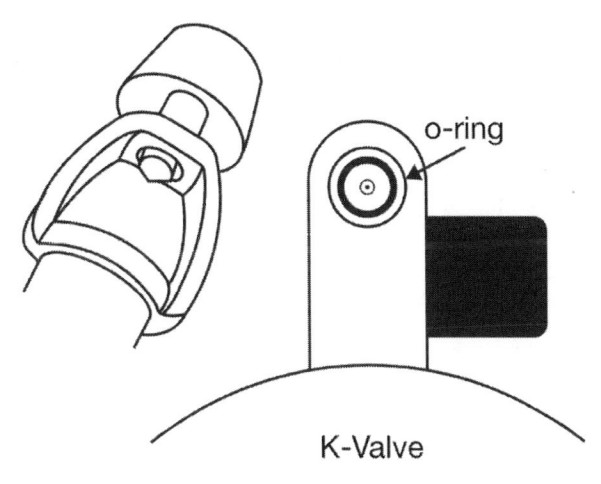

Figure 27 Tank valves

Key things to remember:

Tanks are made from steel (3AA) or aluminium (3AL). Steel is stronger and has a higher working pressure. Aluminium is more buoyant and less rusty. Tanks have a safety valve called a burst disk, that opens at 140% of the working pressure. Once a year, a tanks needs a visual inspection, where the tank is checked for rust and the O-ring between the tank and the valve that stops rusting caused by galvanic action lubricated or replaced. Depending on local regulations, a hydrostatic test is required every three to seven years. The tank is filled with water and pressurised to 160% of the working pressure, and the amount of expansion of the tank walls is measured. If the tank passes the test, it gets a stamp with the test date and a + if it is ok to fill it 10% higher than the normal working pressure. If not, it is destroyed. Tanks come with a K valve/yoke, a DIN valve, or an old J valve, that has a 50 Bar warning mechanism.

REGULATORS

The first stage and the second stage.
Balanced and unbalanced. Environmental seals.
Failsafe designs, upstream and downstream.
The Venturi system.

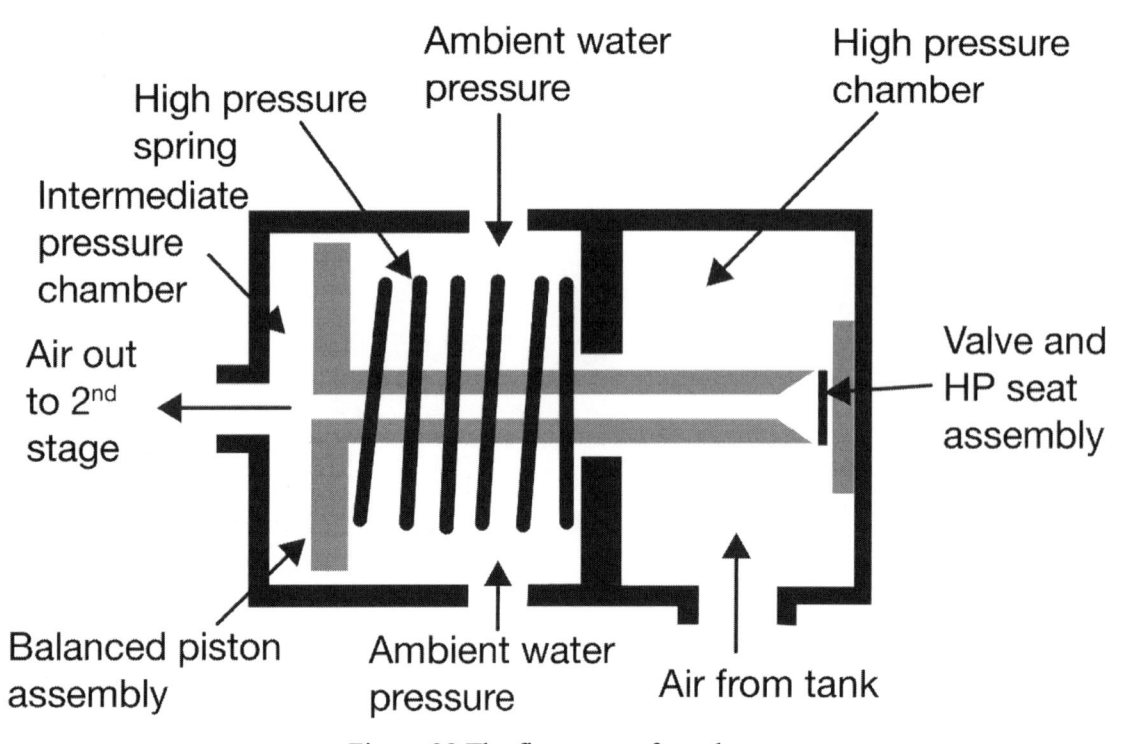

Figure 28 The first stage of regulator

The first regulators were closed circuit rebreathers (closed circuit scuba). The air was circulated through a device that the scrubbed the oxygen from your exhaled carbon dioxide so that you can use the oxygen again. A semi-closed circuit (semi-closed scuba) was also commonly used (and is becoming popular again), in which a small amount of air is constantly enriched with extra oxygen and released into the circuit, and some of the used air is allowed to escape. But by far the most popular system is the open circuit scuba, which is what you will be familiar with.

The air, under high pressure in the tank, is lowered to the ambient pressure by a regulator, and the air you breathe out is simply released. It supplies air only when you inhale, by using a demand valve. Modern regulators have two stages. The regulator first stage, the one you attach to the tank, lowers the air to intermediate pressure (around 9 Bar above the ambient pressure), and the second stage that you hold in your mouth, reduces the pressure to ambient pressure.

Your first stage has 2 chambers: a high pressure chamber that feeds air with tank pressure to the intermediate pressure chamber. Here, the pressure is lowered to about 9 -13 bar above the ambient water pressure. The intermediate pressure chamber is open to the water at the ambient pressure. It has small holes. When you inhale, the air pressure in intermediate pressure chamber drops below the ambient pressure, causing the water to push in. The water moves a diaphragm or a piston. This opens a valve to allow air to flow in from the high pressure chamber. The air keeps flowing as long as the diver inhales, and the pressure stays lower than intermediate pressure. When diver stops inhaling, the pressure rises in the intermediate chamber until it reaches intermediate pressure. Now the valve closes and air no longer flows until the diver inhales again.

From the intermediate pressure chamber, the air flows to your second stage. Here, the intermediate air pressure is lowered to ambient pressure. The second stage has a valve that lets the air in from the tank, and another valve that opens when you exhale to blow the air into the water. When you inhale, the valve that lets air out is closed – otherwise you would inhale water! This means you suck the air out of the second stage, and the pressure drops below ambient pressure. This moves a diaphragm that opens a valve that allows air to flow from the first stage into the second stage. When you exhale, the pressure in the second stage gets higher than ambient pressure, and this pushes out the diaphragm and closes the valve that lets air in. At the same time it opens valve that lets air out. See Figure 28.

On a simple first stage, the water simply goes into a special chamber where it acts on the piston or diaphragm and springs. In a first stage with an environmental seal, the water does not come into contact with any moving parts, but pushes against a silicone liquid or alcohol seal, which then transfers the pressure to the internal mechanism. The advantage of an environmental seal is that your first stage stays cleaner, and most importantly, that it doesn't freeze up in cold water. So, a regulator can have an environmental seal, or it may not do. A first stage may also be a balanced first stage or an unbalanced first stage. In a simple unbalanced first stage, the spring system works with the pressure from your tank. If the pressure is less (tank empty), or if you require more air (deep dive, buddy breathing to your tank with it), it becomes harder to breathe. In a balanced first stage the spring system is designed so that it is independent of the pressure in your tank. It takes a lot more springs to achieve this, but breathing comfort always remains the same. Unbalanced regulators are fine for shallow recreational diving, and are easy to maintain. The rental regulators from diving schools are often unbalanced. Balanced regulators are more comfortable, but more expensive and harder to maintain. They are often used by serious divers and dive professionals.

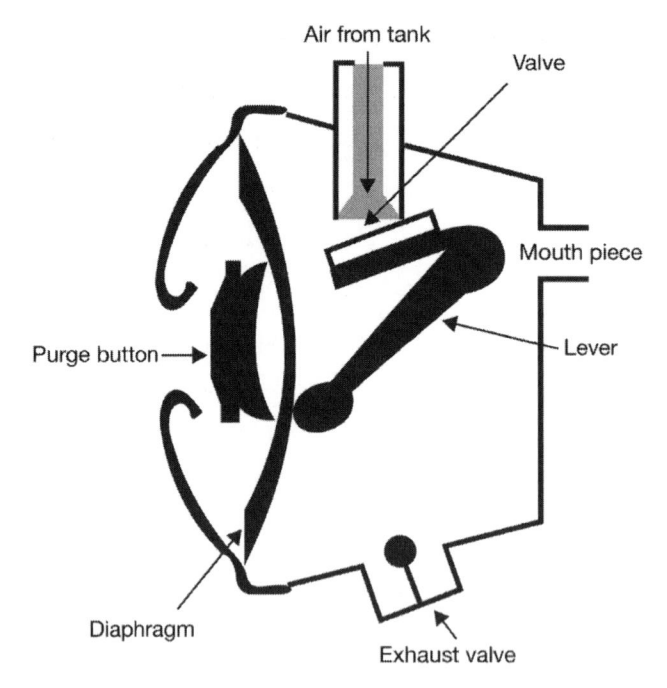

Figure 29 The second stage of a regulator

Now let's have a look to the regulator second stage in Figure 29. This is a very simple design, it gives only air when you demand air from it: it's a demand valve. It is basically a plastic cup that is open at the bottom. The pressure on the inside is always equal to the pressure on the outside, because it is open. The first stage provides air to your second stage. The entrance is closed by a piston with a spring. This spring is connected to a membrane. When you inhale you suck the membrane upwards, and this opens the spring and therefore the air supply. If you do not breathe, the spring keeps the air valve closed. As it is described here, you have a system that opens with the flow (downstream). Simple, and if anything breaks, the air valve will open automatically and will start free flowing rather than close off the air. This makes it safe in case it breaks, we call this failsafe. Some of the more expensive second stages have systems that open against the flow (upstream). So they need an auxiliary valve, a pilot valve, which opens the real valve that opens the air stream. They breathe easier, but they are not failsafe, and they are harder to maintain. In addition, some second stages come with a dial that controls how much air they give. Do not confuse this with a Venturi system switch. A Venturi system is a piece of plastic that disturbs the airflow around the diaphragm. This causes the air to swirl in the second stage, creating local low pressure, and making it easier to suck up the diaphragm. A Venturi system can be turned to plus or minus. On the surface it should be set to minus, otherwise your second stages might start free flowing. Under water you should turn the valve to plus on your primary second stage, to make breathing easier and more efficient.

A last remark about diving with air with a high percentage of oxygen. Oxygen is aggressive stuff, and corrodes things easily, or sets them on fire. When you go diving with air containing more than 40% oxygen, your gear must be oxygen clean, and special material must be used for the O-rings and the lubricant. And as a reminder, if you dive with enriched air, the oxygen percentage must be clearly marked on the tank along with your name and the maximum depth, you should have green and yellow bands on your tank and a visual inspection sticker for enriched air (which also states if the tank is suitable or not) and last but not least, you must personally verify the oxygen percentage before you go diving. Tanks with pure oxygen are totally green or white, and have an "Oxygen" sticker.

Key things to remember:

Regulators are closed circuit, semi closed circuit or the most popular: open circuit. The first stage of an open circuit brings the tank pressure down to an intermediate pressure of about 9 Bars above the ambient pressure. They have an environmental seal or not, and they are balanced or not. An environmental seal stops the first stage from getting dirty or freezing up. A balanced regulator maintains the same breathing ease, no matter how high the demand or how low the supply is, an unbalanced regulator does not. The second stage brings the air pressure back to ambient pressure. It is demand valve that is usually constructed to open with the air flow (downstream), but sometimes it open against the air flow (upstream). An upstream valve needs a pilot valve to open up against the air flow. All second stages have Venturi system that helps to open the main valve. It should be off on the surface to prevent free flowing.

Find out more:

http://en.wikipedia.org/wiki/Diving_regulator

DEPTH GAUGES

Capillary depth gauges, theoretical depths and for altitude diving. Open and closed Bourdon tubes. Electrical systems: transducers.

The simplest depth gauge is not much more than a glass that you hold opening down in the water. This is a capillary depth gauge. The air space will be become smaller as you descend (Boyle's Law!) and the water level will rise in the glass So, at a known depth, you mark where the water is now. You take it to the next known depth, and you mark where the water is again. You can then take it on a dive where the depth is not previously known and the gauge can tell you how deep you are. The problem with such a depth gauge is that the marks get closer together the deeper you go, because the pressure differences are becoming smaller as you go deeper (as you learned earlier). They come in handy when diving at altitude. At altitude you must plan you dives as if you are diving deeper than you are to allow for bigger pressure differences between the surface and depth. If you have calibrated a capillary depth gauge at sea level, and then use it in a mountain lake, it will indicate that you are deeper than you actually are. This is because of the surface pressure differences at altitudes higher than at sea level. The pressure at the surface at sea level is 1 Bar. At 10 metres deep you have two (1+1) Bar, twice as much as the surface, so the air space in the gauge will be half the size. But if you start with say, 0.5 Bar at the surface in a very high and very cold mountain lake, at 10 meters there be 1.5 Bar (1+0.5). This is three times as much.as the pressure at the surface (which was 0.5 Bar), and so the air will be a third in size: your capillary pressure gauge will indicate that you're at twenty metres (3 bars at sea level) while you're only at ten. It will indicate approximately the theoretical depths that you work out with altitude tables.

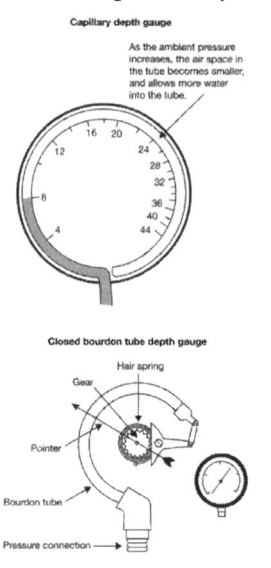

Figure 30 Depth gauges

Another kind of depth gauge is the open or closed bourdon tube. This is a flexible tube in the shape of a C, containing gas or liquid that is in contact with the ambient pressure. The higher the pressure, the more the tube straightens. The tube is connected to gears and levers, which is connected to a needle that moves around a dial that tells you how deep you are. If the tube is protected from the water through a barrier of oil or a membrane it is closed bourdon tube. If it is open, it is an open bourdon tube! See Figure 30. Open bourdon tubes have problems with rust. Accuracy remains a problem in all analogue depth gauges. Digital depth gauges are however extremely accurate. These you will find in your dive computer. It consists of a simple transducer: a tiny electrical current is introduced one side of a piece of porcelain with air bubbles in it. Porcelain does not conduct electricity, but the bubbles do conduct the current. The deeper you go, the more the bubbles are compressed, and less current is conducted. This way you can determine the depth very accurately.

Key things to remember:

Capillary depth gauges are open systems that show depth by showing a change in volume. They show depth relative to the surface pressure: theoretical depths. This makes them suitable for altitude diving. A disadvantage is that they become less accurate at increasing depths. A bourdon tube works on the same principle, but the pressure straightens a tube connected with clogs to a pointer. Bourdon tubes are open, or closed. A transducer determines depth by measuring the strength of an electric current conducted through porcelain in which the resistance increases at depth because of the compression of the tiny air bubbles in it.

Find out more: http://en.wikipedia.org/wiki/Pressure_measurement

THE PHYSIOLOGY OF DIVING

How does your body react to diving? How does the increased pressure affect you? What are the effects of breathing compressed air? To be able to answer these questions you need to understand how the major body systems work. We first look at blood and the cardiovascular system, your lungs and respiration, oxygen and carbon dioxide. We will have a look at the effects of oxygen and nitrogen under pressure, gas narcosis and decompression sickness. Next, we look at some possible problems in diving: risk of decompression sickness, lung over-expansion injuries, ear and sinus barotraumas, and temperature problems.

BLOOD. OXYGEN, CARBON DIOXIDE AND CARBON MONOXIDE

Cellular respiration.
Red blood cells and plasma.
Haemoglobine.
Carbon monoxide poisoning.

Every cell in your body needs oxygen. This process, called cellular respiration, is just your cells using oxygen to 'burn' food for energy, and like a real fire, carbon dioxide is produced as a waste product. It is the job of your lungs, heart and circulatory system to transport oxygen to your cells, and to remove carbon dioxide. Blood is a fluid, of course, and the fluid itself is called plasma. There is some oxygen dissolved in the plasma (as with any liquid that is in contact with air), but it is not enough to provide the body cells with the oxygen they need. In fact, the blood plasma can only transport about two percent of the oxygen you need. Therefore, there are special cells called red blood cells floating the plasma whose only job it is to transport oxygen. About a quarter of all your cells in your body are red blood cells (there are a staggering 20.000.000.000 red blood cells in your body). The reason these cells are so good at transporting oxygen is that they contain haemoglobin (in Greek the word 'haîma' means blood and 'globus' means sphere). Haemoglobin is an excellent substance for transporting oxygen because it binds very easily with oxygen when the partial pressure of oxygen is high, as it is in your lungs. However, when the partial pressure of oxygen is low, as it is in your cells as a result of cellular respiration, haemoglobin releases the oxygen. Your cells can then use the oxygen, and the oxygen-depleted red blood cells go back to your lungs, where they 'reload' and circulate again, see Figure 31. (Again, there are a staggering 270.000.000 molecules of haemoglobin inside EACH ONE of your

20.000.000.000 red blood cells. They are so full of it that they do not even have DNA inside it. You don't have to remember these numbers, as long as you go: WOW!) You can see if blood is high in oxygen or low in oxygen from its colour. When the red blood cells coming from the heart and the lungs are oxygenated, the blood is bright red, when they are deoxygenated, coming from the rest of the body, the blood is dark red. The majority of waste carbon dioxide is carried away from the cells dissolved in the blood plasma itself (in the form of bicarbonate), though a small amount does also bond with haemoglobin, around ten percent to be exact. It is actually the ions that are left when carbon monoxide turns into bicarbonate that make the oxygen pop off haemoglobin, a perfect system: when there is a lot of carbon dioxide red blood cells give up a lot of oxygen.

In the lungs, where the partial pressure is high, oxygen bonds easily with the haemogloblin in the red blood cells. Oxygen is then transported to the tissues.

In the tissues, where the partial pressure is low, oxygen unbonds with haemoglobin. The red blood cells then return to the lungs to reload and circulate again.

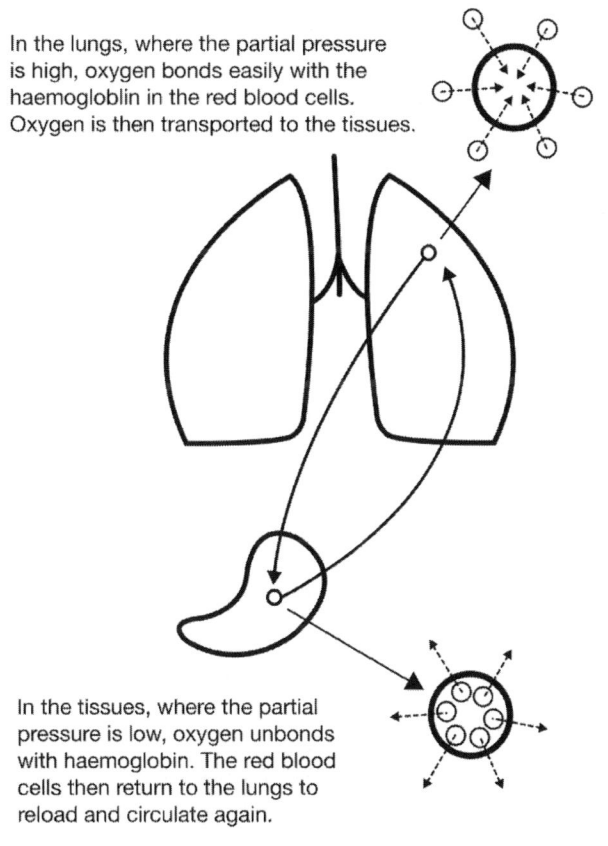

Figure 31 Haemoglobine at work in the blood

In the physics of diving we talked briefly about the poisonous gas carbon monoxide. When fuels, such as oil, gas, coal and wood burn without enough oxygen, carbon monoxide is produced. This is called incomplete combustion. Importantly for divers, it can be produced by the compressors that fill our tanks or the engines of our boats. Carbon monoxide is also produced by cigarette smoke.

Carbon monoxide is dangerous because it is poisonous but tasteless and odourless, so you will have no initial warning of its presence. It is poisonous because it binds with haemoglobin 200 times more easily than oxygen, and, unlike oxygen, it does not unbind. It stays attached to the haemoglobine forever. Your body can never again use the red blood cells that have bound with carbon monoxide, it has to make extra new red blood cells to replace them. It takes eight to twelve hours of breathing fresh air for everything to return to normal. If you continue to breathe carbon monoxide, after a while, there will not enough free haemoglobin to bind with oxygen and therefore your blood will not be able to transport enough oxygen to your tissues. You choke as you breathe. Blood saturated with carbon monoxide is a very bright red, so you can also recognize carbon monoxide poisoning from very red lips and nail beds. Of course, this is difficult to see underwater because of colour absorption.

Carbon monoxide poisoning gives divers symptoms of hypoxia (not enough oxygen) including headache, dizziness, nausea, confusion, light-headedness and numbness. Unfortunately divers are unlikely to notice these warnings diving at depth, because the high partial pressure of oxygen in the air you breathe from your tank is enough to supply them with the sufficient oxygen. However, going up, the partial pressure of the oxygen decreases, while the levels of carbon monoxide remain high. If there are not enough free red blood cells, divers may even blackout from a lack of oxygen.

You should make sure that there is no risk of carbon monoxide being present in your tank. You should always know where your tank has been filled, and you should ensure that the compressor used for filling has been properly maintained and that the intake is not exposed to engine fumes etc. Smoking cigarettes immediately before and after a dive is not a good idea. If you suspect someone of having carbon monoxide poisoning, have them breathe 100 percent oxygen and get medical attention.

Key things to remember:

Every cell in your body needs oxygen for cellular respiration – the process of transferring energy from food to a useable form. Your blood plasma contains red blood cells, that carry oxygen attached to haemoglobin, a substance that binds with oxygen at a high partial pressure (as it is in your lungs), and releases it when the partial pressure is low (as it is in your cells). Carbon dioxide dissolves in the form of a bicarbonate in your blood plasma and is carried away from your cells. Oxygenated blood is bright red, oxygen-poor blood is dark red. Carbon monoxide binds with haemoglobin over 200 times more easily than oxygen, and it does not unbind, meaning that the haemoglobin cannot transport sufficient oxygen to your cells. This can lead to unconsciousness and death. At depth you may not notice the signs and symptoms of carbon monoxide poisoning because of the high partial pressure of oxygen. Give victims of carbon monoxide poisoning pure oxygen.

Find out more:

http://en.wikipedia.org/wiki/Blood
http://en.wikipedia.org/wiki/Hemoglobin
http://en.wikipedia.org/wiki/Carbon_monoxide_poisoning

[A long video that explains it all in depth](#)

THE CARDIOVASCULAR SYSTEM

The heart, veins and arteries.
Baroreceptors and the carotid sinus reflex.

The word 'cardiovascular' refers to your heart and circulatory (blood vessels) system (in Greek the word 'kardia' means heart, and in Latin the word 'vascularis' refers to vessels or tubes). Your heart pumps blood around your body to transport oxygen from your lungs to body cells. An artery is a blood vessel that comes from the heart, a vein is a blood vessel that goes towards the heart. Your heart consists of four chambers, the top two chambers are called the left atrium and the right atrium, and the two bottom chambers are called the left ventricle and the right ventricle. Look at Figure 32.

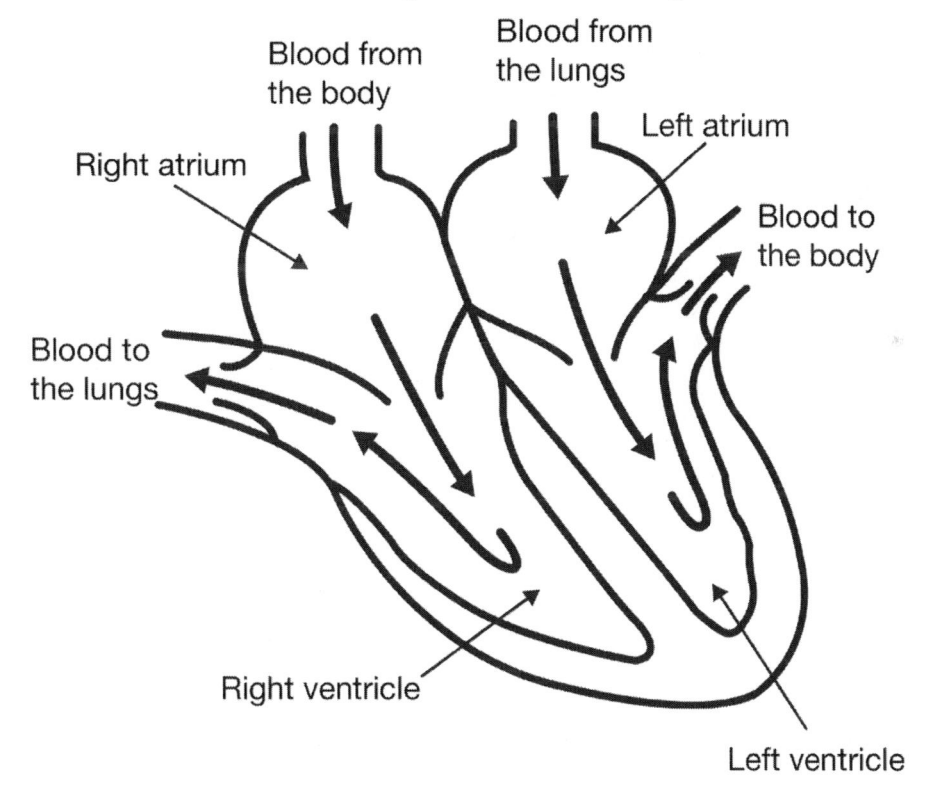

Figure 32 The heart

Now follow the blood. The right side of the heart receives dark red de-oxygenated blood from your organs and the left side of the heart receives re-oxygenated blood from your lungs. Your heart contracts in two stages. Blood is received by your right and left atria, which then contract together and pump blood to the right and left ventricles. Then the ventricles contract together and propel blood out of the heart.

This means the ventricles are stronger than the atria, because they have to pump the blood out of the heart. The right ventricle pumps the blood through the pulmonary artery to the lungs. The pulmonary artery splits into smaller and smaller blood vessels in the lungs that end with hair-like vessels called pulmonary capillaries. The blood picks up oxygen and gets rid of carbon dioxide. The blood then returns to your heart through your pulmonary vein to the left atrium, where it is pumped to your left ventricle. The left ventricle pumps the blood through the aorta, the main artery, to the rest of the body. This means that the left side of the heart is stronger than the right side: the left side has to pump the blood through you whole body, the right side only to your lungs. Your arteries branch into smaller and smaller vessels that end with tiny hair-like blood vessels called capillaries. They are so small that red blood cells actually have to squeeze through! Gas exchange takes place between your capillaries and your tissue cells: oxygen is released and carbon dioxide is picked up. Your veins then take the dark red oxygen-poor blood back to your heart, through the vena cava, the main vein in the body. It enters the right atrium and is pumped to the right ventricle to begin the circulation again. See Figure 33

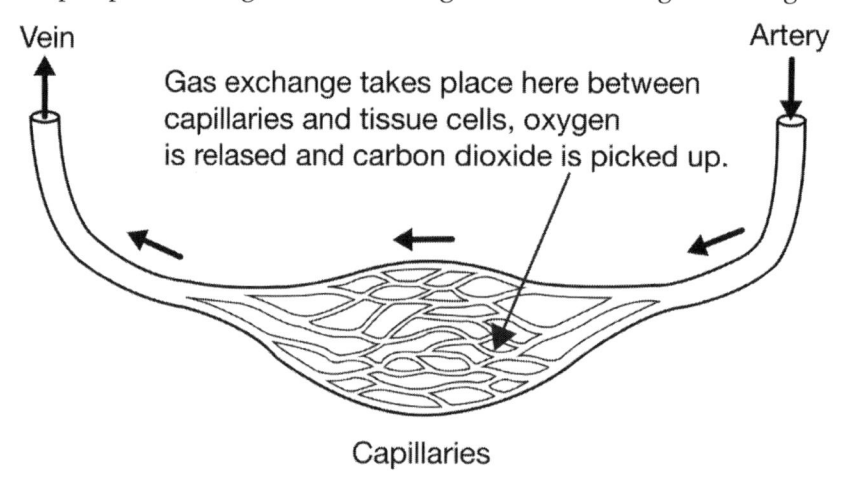

Figure 33 Arteries, capillaries, veins and gas exchange.

The pressure in your arteries is highest during a heartbeat, this is called systolic blood pressure (the word 'systole' means the normal rhythmical contraction of the heart – systole in Greek means 'a drawing up' or a contraction). The pressure is lowest in between heartbeats, this is called diastolic blood pressure (the word 'diastolic' refers to the time when the heart is filling with blood and is in a state of relaxation and expansion – diastole is Greek for 'a drawing apart'). You can see this in Figure 34 Your heart rate is controlled by your brain, responding to baroreceptors that detect pressure in particular arteries ('baro-' means pressure) by measuring how far the artery wall is stretched. If the blood pressure is too high the heart rate decreases, and if it is too low the heart rate increases.

There are important baroreceptors in the arteries that supply your brain with blood: the carotid arteries in your neck. An overly tight-fitting hood or exposure suit can compress the carotid arteries, and cause your brain to be fooled in thinking the blood pressure is high. This will cause your heart rate to slow unnecessarily. If the constriction continues your brain will continue to slow your heart rate which can lead to a loss consciousness due to hypoxia. This is called the carotid sinus reflex. An overly tight-fitting hood or wetsuit can also compress the jugular veins, which return blood from the brain to the heart. This is called a blocked jugular venous return and can cause a dangerous build-up of blood in the brain. Therefore it is very important to ensure that hoods and wetsuits are not too tight around your neck.

Heart contraction - blood is pumped from the ventricles to the body and lungs - pressure in arteries is the highest.

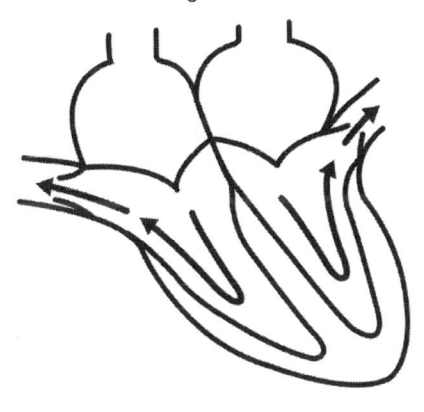

Heart relaxation and expansion (inbetween heart beats) - the heart fills with blood from the body and lungs - pressure in arteries is the lowest.

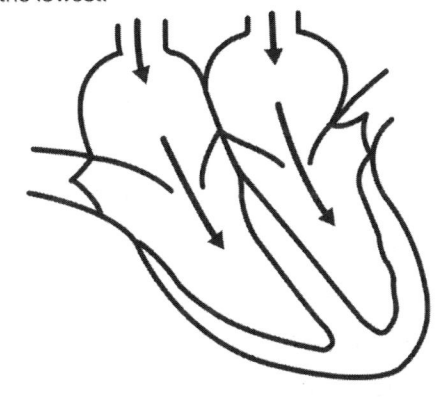

Figure 34 Blood pressure systole and diastole and heart contraction

Key things to remember:

Your heart pumps blood around your circulatory system to transport oxygen from your lungs to your tissue cells. The right side of the heart receives de-oxygenated blood from your organs and the left side of the heart receives oxygenated blood from your lungs. The right side then pumps blood to your lungs to pick up oxygen and get rid of carbon dioxide, and the left side pumps blood to your tissue cells to deliver oxygen and pick up carbon dioxide. Bright red oxygen-rich blood is transported to your organs via your arteries, which branch into smaller and smaller vessels. Your arteries end in very fine hair-like blood vessels called capillaries, which is where gas exchange of oxygen and carbon dioxide takes place. Dark red oxygen poor blood is then transported back to your heart via your veins. Your heart rate is controlled by your brain, which responds to baroreceptors that detect blood pressure in particular arteries. If the blood pressure is too high the heart rate decreases, and if it is too low the heart rate increases. An overly tight-fitting hood or exposure suit can compress the carotid arteries and jugular veins in the neck. This can trigger the carotid-sinus reflex, which is when the brain falsely detects high blood pressure and slows the heart rate, and blocked jugular venous return, which is a dangerous build-up of oxygen poor blood in the brain. This can lead to unconsciousness and death.

Find out more:

http://en.wikipedia.org/wiki/Heart

http://en.wikipedia.org/wiki/Blood_vessel

http://en.wikipedia.org/wiki/Carotid_sinus

Lungs

Trachea, bronchi, bronchioles, alveoli and pulmonary capillaries.

Gas exchange and dead airspace

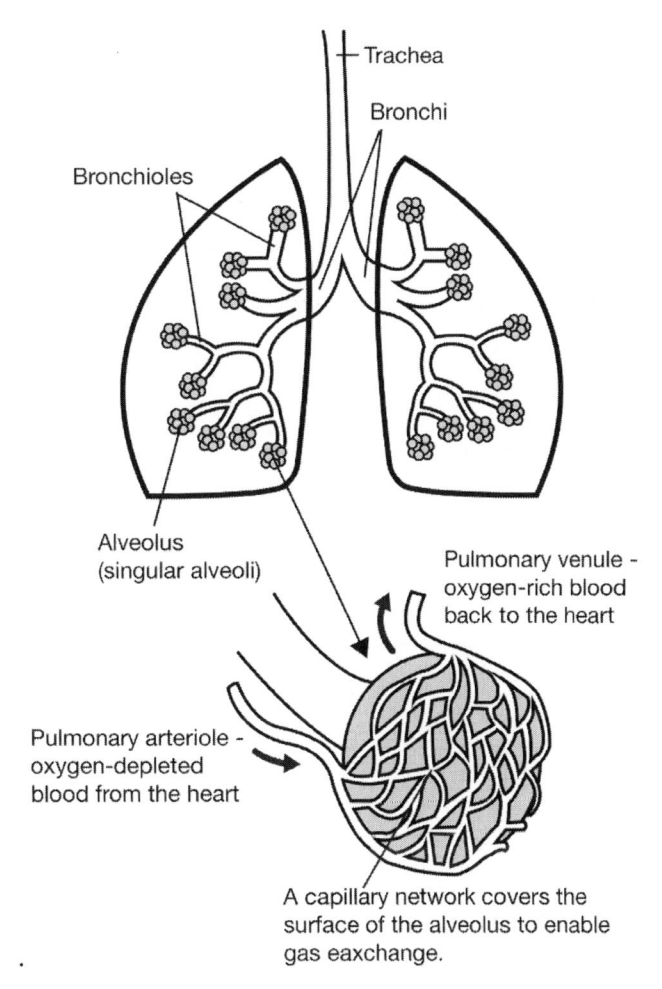

Figure 35 Respiratory system, alveoli and pulmonary capillaries

Your lungs are like sponges: they are soft, expandable and light in a similar way. When you take a breath air first enters your trachea (wind pipe), the trachea then splits into two 'tubes' called your bronchi, which lead to each of your lungs. Within the lungs the bronchi branch into smaller and smaller 'tubes' called your bronchioles. At the end of each bronchiole is very small air sac called an alveolus (alveolus is singular, alveoli is plural). See Figure 355.

The walls of the alveoli (called membranes) between the blood in the pulmonary capillaries and the air in your lungs are very thin. That means that gas exchange can take place easily. Of course, this means that the membrane is very fragile, and we will come back to this point when we talk about lung overexpansion injuries. Together, the lungs contain approximately 2,400 kilometres of airways and 300 to 500 million alveoli, with a total surface area of about 70 square metres to 100 square metres! That's a lot of area for gas exchange to take place!

An important thing to note is that when you exhale some air remains in your mouth, throat and trachea. These areas are called dead air space. The air in your dead air space, which is low in oxygen and high in carbon dioxide, is the first air to enter your lungs on the next inhalation. When we are diving or snorkelling we increase that dead air space with our regulator or snorkel, so it is important to compensate for the extra dead air space by breathing more deeply than usual.

Key things to remember:

Your trachea branches into two bronchi which lead to each of your lungs. In your lungs your bronchi branch into bronchioles, which end in very small air sacs with thin membranes called alveoli. The pulmonary capillaries are in contact with the alveoli, and this is where the gas exchange of oxygen and carbon dioxide takes place. The first air to enter your lungs when you breathe in is air from your previous exhalation that sits in your dead air space (mouth, throat and trachea), this air is low in oxygen and high in carbon dioxide. We must breathe deeply enough to take in fresh air as well. When we dive or snorkel, the regulator or snorkel increases dead air space, meaning that we should breath more deeply than usual.

Find out more:

http://en.wikipedia.org/wiki/Human_lung

RESPIRATION, OXYGEN AND CARBON DIOXIDE

Breathing reflex and hypercapnea.
Hyperventilation and shallow-water black-out.
The Mammelian Reflex.

Let's start by defining some terms that you need to know. The hypo- before a word means too little of something, and the hyper- means too much of something (in Greek 'hypo' is low and 'hyper' is high). Hyperventilation is a term that you have probably heard of, it means you are breathing too quickly. Hypoventilation on the other hand means that you are breathing too slowly. We have previously mentioned the term hypoxia, which means that levels of oxygen in your body are too low. Hyperoxia is when levels of oxygen are too high. When levels of carbon dioxide are too low we call that hypocapnia, and when they are too high we call that hypercapnia ('oxia' means oxygen, and capnia means carbon dioxide). Brady means slow and tachy means quick. So a slow heartbeat is bradycardia, and a quick heartbeat is tachycardia.

You breathe to get oxygen to your cells. You can control your breathing consciously, but for the most part your brain does it without you, unconsciously. Strangely enough, the urge to breath is not triggered by low levels of oxygen, as would be logical, but by high levels of carbon dioxide in your blood. Now let's talk about hypercapnia and hypocapnia.

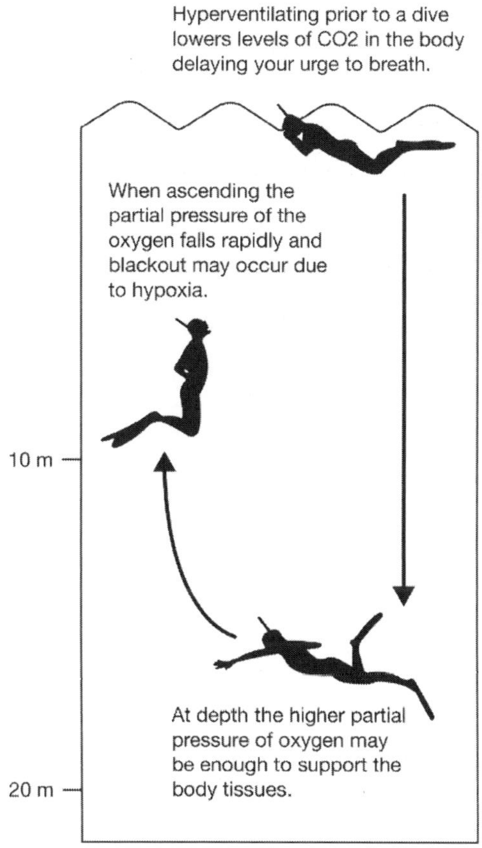

Hyperventilating prior to a dive lowers levels of CO2 in the body delaying your urge to breath.

When ascending the partial pressure of the oxygen falls rapidly and blackout may occur due to hypoxia.

10 m

At depth the higher partial pressure of oxygen may be enough to support the body tissues.

20 m

Figure 36 Shallow water black out

How do we divers suffer hypercapnia? The most frequent cause is to take shallow breaths. Your inhalations will come from your dead air space, and that air contains a lot of carbon dioxide. Shallow breathing can occur if you overexert yourself, or simply because you don't adopt a good breathing pattern. To make things worse, carbon dioxide will build up in your blood and trigger you to breathe more frequently and shallowly, which can lead to a cycle that makes you feel starved for air.

A second way in which divers experience hypercapnia, is by holding your breath too long before exhaling, in the belief that it will help you to conserve air (skip breathing). This is not the case, in the period you are holding your breath carbon dioxide builds up, and you simply start breathing faster and shallower. Thirdly, when you dive with a semi-closed or closed-circuit rebreather, it can malfunction and fail to remove carbon dioxide before feeding air back into the loop. This can be very serious, and it is part of the training to spot these problems before and during a dive. Finally, if you are free diving or even just duck-diving when snorkelling (referred to as apnea diving, which simply means breath-hold diving: in Greek 'a' means not and pneuma means air) your body accumulates higher levels of carbon dioxide during the time you are holding your breath, and so you should take adequate rest of the surface between dives. And remember, of course, when snorkelling to take deep breaths to breath past the extra dead air space created by the snorkel.

Initial signs and symptoms of hypercapnia are rapid breathing (remember that the term for that is hyperventilation), shortness of breath, rapid heartbeat (tachycardia – 'tachy' means fast and kardia means 'heart'), headache and excessive sweating; higher levels of carbon dioxide will lead to mental impairment and unconsciousness.

We mentioned that you can suffer from hypercapnia when apnea diving, but you can also have problems resulting from hypocapnea (too little carbon dioxide). It is possible to extend your breath-hold time by taking three to four quick deep breaths (so to deliberately hyperventilate) before you make a dive. This lowers the level of carbon dioxide in your blood and suppresses your urge to breathe. But you have to be very careful! You can suppress the urge to breathe by lowering the level of carbon dioxide in your blood too far. That means you can hold your breath longer than is good for you. Now, while you are at depth the higher partial pressure of the oxygen in your blood plasma might be enough to support your tissues, but when you go up, the partial pressure of the oxygen falls rapidly. There is simply not enough oxygen for your brain and you black out due to hypoxia. This is the famous shallow water blackout. See Figure 36. This is serious because you will drown if there is no one there to bring you up to the surface or get your face out of the water. This really is a danger that you should never underestimate. Doing a dive holding your breath seems so easy and safe for us divers. It is not. Always practice apnea diving with a buddy and never excessively hyperventilate before a dive.

One more thing to talk about is the mammalian reflex. This is what happens: 1) when the face is underwater the heart rate immediately slows to conserve oxygen - in humans the heart rate slows down 10 to 20 percent, in seals the heart rate slows to as low as 10 beats per minute; 2) the blood vessels in your legs, arms, hands, and feet contract (this is called vasoconstriction – 'veso' is Latin for vessel) leaving more blood for the heart and brain; 3) (during very deep dives only) blood plasma fills the chest cavity so that the lungs are not crushed by the pressure – in humans during this stage of the reflex blood plasma fills your alveoli and has been observed on apnea dives deeper than 90 metres. The mammalian reflex is strong in aquatic mammals such as seals, dolphins and otters, but it also present in land mammals, including us. Children exhibit it more strongly than adults. The reflex is only triggered in water colder than 21°C and only when the face is submerged in the water.

Key things to remember:

Your urge to breath is not triggered by a depletion of oxygen, but by the build-up of carbon dioxide in your blood. The prefix hypo- means too little of something, and the prefix hyper- means too much of something. Hyperventilation means you are breathing too quickly. Hypoventilation on the other hand means that you are breathing too slowly. Hypoxia means that levels of oxygen in your body are too low. Hyperoxia is when levels of oxygen are too high. When levels of carbon dioxide are too low we call that hypocapnia, and when they are too high we call that hypercapnia. There are a few ways in which you can be affected by hypercapnia: by taking shallow breaths due to overexertion or a bad breathing pattern, from skip breathing, from a malfunctioning rebreather, and from taking insufficient breaths between apnea dives. Initial signs and symptoms of hypercapnia are hyperventilation, shortness of breath, tachycardia, headache and excessive sweating; higher levels of carbon dioxide will lead to mental impairment and unconsciousness. If you excessively hyperventilate before an apnea dive you can suffer a shallow water blackout. You suppress the urge to breathe by lowering the level of carbon dioxide in your blood too far, and you stay under water too long. Underwater, the oxygen in your blood plasma is usable because of the high partial pressure, but when you go up the partial pressure of the oxygen falls rapidly, causing you to black out due to hypoxia. Always take a buddy. The mammalian reflex is present in all mammals, though it is much more pronounced in aquatic mammals, and helps to extend breath-hold time in water of below 21°C with the face submerged in the water. It works by slowing the heart rate and vasoconstriction to preserve oxygen, and at greater depths by filling the chest cavity with blood plasma to prevent the lungs being crushed by the pressure.

Find out more:

http://en.wikipedia.org/wiki/Lung

http://en.wikipedia.org/wiki/Hyperventilation

http://en.wikipedia.org/wiki/Freediving

http://en.wikipedia.org/wiki/Mammalian_diving_reflex

THE EFFECTS OF BREATHING OXYGEN UNDER PRESSURE

Pulmonary and Central Nervous System Oxygen Toxicity.

When you are diving you breathe oxygen and nitrogen with a higher pressure than at the surface. We need oxygen to live, but too much oxygen is bad for you. Your body cannot handle breathing air with a high percentage or high partial pressure of oxygen for a long time. The oxygen irritates your airways and lungs, so we call this Pulmonary Oxygen Toxicity. Your body cannot handle a high partial pressure of oxygen (getting to much oxygen per breath) either. The oxygen affects your central nervous system causing convulsions, so we call this Central Nervous System Oxygen Toxicity. First let's look at

Pulmonary Oxygen Toxicity. As we have previously mentioned the partial pressure of the oxygen you normally breathe at the surface at sea level is 0.21 Bar. If you breathe oxygen of a partial pressure of higher than 0.5 Bar over an extended period of time it irritates first your trachea and bronchi, followed by your bronchioles and alveoli. It will cause a burning sensation in your throat and lungs, and frequent coughing. The higher the pressure of the oxygen the more quickly it will cause irritation. Breathing 100 percent oxygen at 1 Bar of pressure (sea level) can cause irritation after around 6 to 9 hours. If you have ever known anyone in hospital who is breathing 100 percent oxygen, you will have noticed that the patient was periodically given air breaks to allow the lungs to recover and prevent toxicity. If a patient would benefit from higher levels of oxygen over a long period, hospitals will not use 100 percent oxygen but a lower percentage. Pulmonary Oxygen Toxicity is not a problem for recreational divers, because although we do breathe oxygen at partial pressures higher than 0.5 PPO_2, we do not do so over long enough periods of time to suffer any ill effects. It is possible for technical divers to suffer from Pulmonary Oxygen Toxicity because of the long periods of time they spend breathing elevated partial pressures of oxygen.

Now let's look at Central Nervous System Oxygen Toxicity. If you breath oxygen of a partial pressure higher than 1.4 – 1.6 Bar it can affect your central nervous system and lead to convulsions. Convulsions underwater are very, very, dangerous because you are unable to keep your regulator in your mouth and are likely to drown. As we have previously mentioned in the physics of diving, it is not possible to have problems with CNS Oxygen Toxicity within recreational limits breathing normal air, but it is possible when breathing enriched air Nitrox. When diving with Nitrox always stay well within your maximum operational depth, which is the depth at which the partial pressure of the oxygen in the blend that you are breathing reaches 1.4 Bar. CNS Oxygen Toxicity is the leading cause of death in technical diving. To calculate your Maximum Operational Depth (MOD) divide 1.4 Bar by the percentage of the oxygen in the Nitrox mix that you are using. For example if you are using EAN38 (Nitrox with 38 percent oxygen):

1.4 PPO_2 ÷ 0.38 = 3.7 Bar (3.7 Bar is the pressure at 27 metres, remember, divide by ten, and one of the atmosphere itself)

Key things to remember:

Breathing oxygen of a partial pressure of higher than 0.5 PPO2 over an extended period of time irritates your lungs, causing a burning sensation in your throat and lungs, and frequent coughing. It is not a problem in recreational diving because dive times are not long enough to cause symptoms. It can be a problem in technical diving. If you breath oxygen at a partial pressure higher than 1.4 – 1.6 Bar it can affect your central nervous system and lead to convulsions.

Convulsions underwater are very dangerous because you are unable to keep your regulator in your mouth and you are likely to drown. It can be a problem within recreational diving limits when using Nitrox.

Find out more:

http://en.wikipedia.org/wiki/Oxygen_toxicity

GAS NARCOSIS

Different gases, different narcotic effect. Signs and symptoms.

Gas narcosis is often called nitrogen narcosis, but that is wrong, because all gases you breathe under pressure have a varying narcotic effect. A gas that dissolves easily in fat is highly narcotic: the more soluble in fat it is, the more narcotic it is. This is probably because the linings of nerve cells are made from fatty substances, and the easier gas can go in, the more narcotic the effect is. Helium is the least soluble, and so the least narcotic, and it is for this reason used in technical diving (Trimix is a blend of oxygen, nitrogen and helium). Gas narcosis of nitrogen usually begins to have an effect at around 30 metres/4 Bar. It can feel like being drunk, resulting in irresponsible behaviour such as failing to monitor your air and depth. But like drugs or alcohol it doesn't always give you a pleasant feeling, it can also make you feel paranoid. Most divers will not feel the effects strongly at 30 metres/4 Bar or even beyond to the recreational limit of 40 metres/5 Bar. However, even if you may not notice it, your reaction times will be slower and your ability to solve problems is impaired. The effects of gas narcosis can be different for different people, and even differ from dive to dive within the same person. Also, if there are traces of alcohol or recreational drugs in your body, or if you are dehydrated, the effect of gas narcosis will be greater.

Carbon dioxide also has a narcotic effect, and so hypercapnia due to overexertion or inefficient breathing will increase the effect of gas narcosis. Panic due to feelings of paranoia can make you start breathing heavily but shallowly and increase levels of carbon dioxide in the blood. A nasty spiral. Fortunately, the solution is always easy and always the same; go up. When you go up, all effects immediately disappear.

Key things to remember:

All gases are narcotic above a certain partial pressure, but some are more narcotic then others. Gas narcosis usually begins to affect you at around 30 metres/4 Bar. It can feel like being drunk, resulting in irresponsible behaviour, but it can also make you feel paranoid. The effects of gas narcosis go away immediately when you go up and the pressure decreases.

Find out more:

http://en.wikipedia.org/wiki/Nitrogen_narcosis

Decompression sickness

Excessive super saturation and gas seeds/micronuclei. Silent bubbles.
Type I decompression sickness: pain only, skin and joints.
Type II decompression sickness: dangerous pulmonary and cerebral symptoms.

When you descend on a dive, the partial pressure of the nitrogen in the air you breathe gets higher and higher, and more and more nitrogen dissolves into your tissues, until they are saturated. When you go up again, and the pressure becomes less, this nitrogen in your tissues now has to come out. The difference in the pressure between two things, like the air and your blood for example is called the pressure gradient). You need to know this term.

As long as you go up slowly, there will be no big bubbles. However, if the difference between the pressure of the nitrogen dissolved in your tissues and the pressure of nitrogen in the air you breathe is too high, it is possible that bubbles form in blood and tissues. This happens when you go up too fast, or when you stay at depth for too long. But it is not quite as simple as that. Bubbles can only get started when there are tiny micro bubbles to form around. These tiny micro bubbles are called 'gas micronuclei' or 'gas seeds. So, if you were to pressurise a glass of pure water, no matter how quickly you released the pressure, no bubbles would form. There is nothing that can act as seeds. However, if you shake the water to make tiny bubbles, seeds, before releasing the pressure, big bubbles can form around them. Of course, your blood is continuously being shaken in the arteries and veins, and so there are many micronuclei available. The quicker your blood flows, the more micronuclei there are, of course. See Figure 37.

Micronuclei or 'gas seeds'

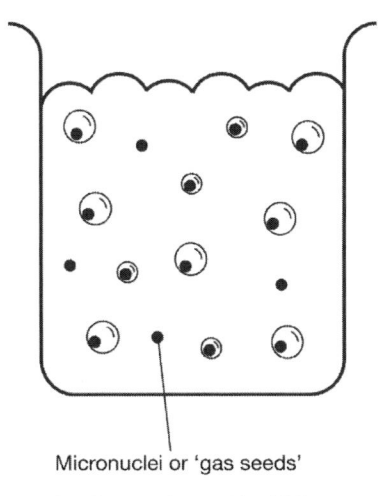

Figure 37 The formation of bubbles

We think that this formation of micro bubbles mainly occurs in the capillaries. During any dive, no matter how shallow or how short, these nitrogen bubbles will be present. This is usually not a problem, because these micro bubbles usually enter the veins and flow back to the heart without causing any blockages. When they reach the pulmonary capillaries in the lungs, they simply diffuse into the alveoli with no problems and you breathe out the nitrogen gas. We call these bubbles 'silent bubbles'. They are there, but they cause no problems. We can see them with the same ultrasound technique that doctors use to show an embryo in a pregnant woman, with a Doppler Ultrasound Flow Meter. This machine is usually pointed at the hearts of people taking part in tests in hyperbaric chambers. These volunteers are pressurised to different pressures for different times, and by measuring the amount of silent bubbles we can see what the safe limits of pressure and time are, without making these people ill. We can make very accurate and safe dive tables this way.

The more nitrogen that is released, the more bubbles grow. So if you make a fast ascent or if you stay too long at depth and accumulate a lot of nitrogen, more nitrogen is trying to leave your tissues as you ascend, making larger bubbles. When bubbles become large they block blood flow in narrow blood vessels, and this makes the problem bigger, because it becomes even more difficult to transport the nitrogen to the lungs. The bubbles become larger and larger, blocking the blood flow more and more. Bubble formation is not limited to the blood, either. Bubbles also form between tissues. They are particularly likely to form in watery tissues, such as tissue that makes up ligaments and joints. As bubbles grow they can also compress nerve cells. Your body's immune system can also make matters worse, because it attacks foreign bodies in the blood by forming platelets around them (the same process as when you have an external wound and platelets cause your blood to clot). This increases the size of the bubble, causing further blockages and irritating surrounding tissue.

The good news is that nitrogen bubbles almost never go into arteries. This is because bubbles come from body tissues, flow through veins back to the heart, and from there they first have to pass the lungs. In the lungs, they usually diffuse through the alveoli, and they are gone before the blood flows back to heart and into the arteries. However, some people (about one quarter of people) have a hole between the left and right sides of their heart. Of course, bubbles can pass through this hole, and miss the lungs. This hole is called a Patent Foramen Ovale (PFO). We are all born with this hole, because in the womb we do not breathe, and so the blood has to circulate without going to the lungs. After birth, this hole normally closes in a few days. If this does not happen perfectly, only a flap of tissue forms over the hole, and these people have a PFO. This does not normally cause problems, they may not even know about it. But if a diver with a PFO has big nitrogen bubbles, they can skip the lungs through the hole, so they do not dissolve, and then they can enter the arteries and travel anywhere in the body, including the brain and cause problems.

Because it takes quite some time for the bubbles to grow and to block things, the signs and symptoms of Decompression sickness don't usually appear immediately after a dive, especially not after recreational dive. In fact, they usually appear a few hours after a dive, even up to 48 hours later. And symptoms often get worse slowly. That's because the bubbles normally need time to grow and cause problems. That is very good news for divers. Most cases of decompression sickness are not immediately life threatening, but, in ALL cases of suspected decompression sickness the diver must go to a doctor.

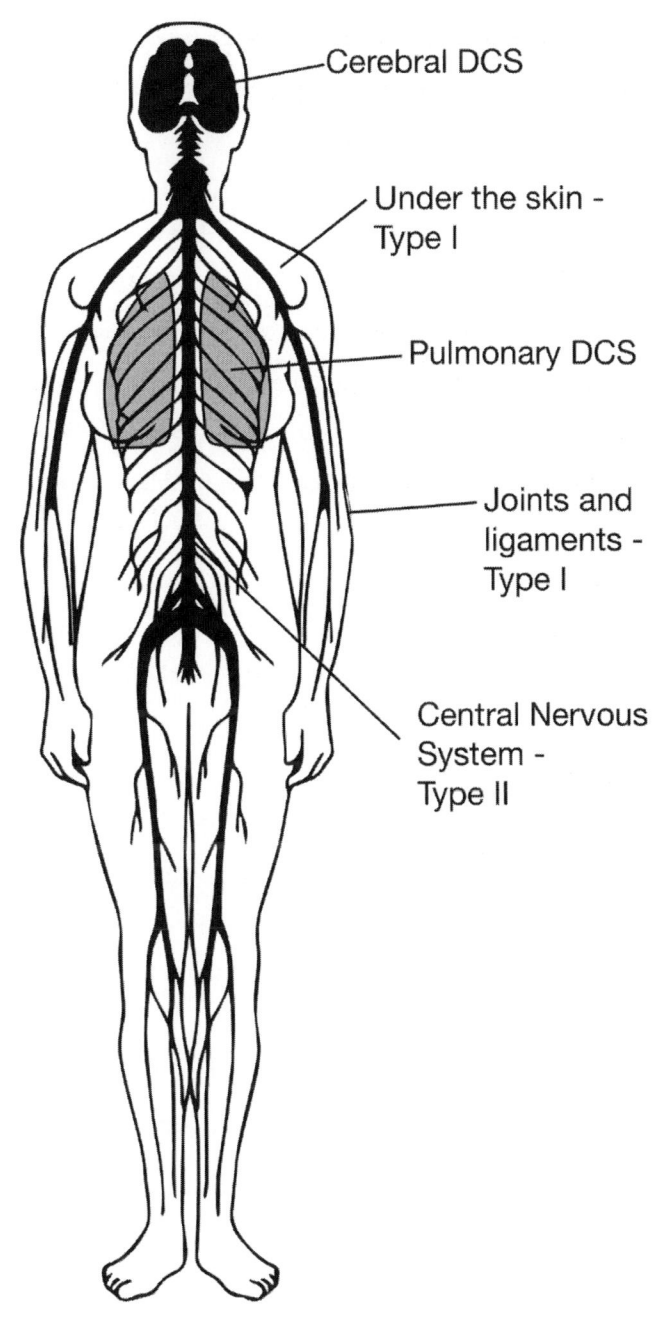

Figure 38 Decompression Sickness Type I and II and locations

Decompression sickness comes in two types. Decompression sickness type I is the least dangerous, and fortunately three quarter of all cases of decompression sickness are this type. The bubbles are not in very dangerous places, usually in the joints, ligaments or under the skin (this last one is called subcutaneous decompression sickness or skin bends). Bubbles under the skin appear as red blotches, and are most frequently under the skin of your shoulders and chest, though they can be anywhere. It is itchy, but it is not serious. If the bubbles are in a joint or ligament they cause pain and make moving that area difficult. Divers with decompression sickness Type I still have to go to a doctor, because the bubbles can get bigger and keep moving, and things may get worse and become decompression sickness type II.

Decompression sickness type II is rare, but serious and can lead to death. The most common form of type II decompression sickness is nitrogen bubbles that interfere with the functioning of your central nervous system. This causes tingling, numbness, loss of bladder control, difficulty with balance and in the worst cases, paralysis. Nitrogen bubbles can very occasionally block blood supply back to your heart, causing your blood pressure to drop too much, leading to unconsciousness. And in very rare cases bubbles are taken back to the heart from the lungs and pumped to your arteries and the rest of your body. If these bubbles end up in the brain, you have a big problem. Nitrogen bubbles can also even form in the brain directly (cerebral decompression sickness) and block blood flow to brain areas. Depending on where this occurs you can experience tunnel vision, dizziness, confusion, and if bubbles block very important areas (for example the area where your heart rate is regulated) it can lead immediately to death. Nitrogen bubbles that affect the lungs (pulmonary decompression sickness) are rare because bubbles usually dissolve in the alveoli, but if there are too many bubbles they cause a blockage. This irritates the lungs, causing shortness of breath and coughing (it is often called the chokes). See Figure 38.

Now this all sounds very scary, but the risk of decompression sickness is very, very small when you dive within the limits of your table or computer. To give you can idea of numbers, the chance of getting decompression sickness on a recreational dive is 1 in 10,000 (see the link below to see how we came to this estimate). And the chances of suffering from life threatening decompression sickness are even smaller. If you follow the rules and stay within the limits, you really have nothing to worry about. Most cases of decompression sickness are caused by diver error, and the majority of cases of decompression sickness occur after technical dives, because these dives are deeper and longer, and there is much more that can go wrong.

Now you may ask, why nitrogen bubbles cause decompression sickness, and not oxygen bubbles? The first reason is that you use oxygen in metabolism, and so it is quickly taken out of the bloodstream by to body cells. This is often given as the only reason, but that's not the full story. The second reason is that the majority of oxygen is attached to your red blood cells rather than dissolved in your blood plasma, so it simply cannot form bubbles. The third reason is that oxygen does not form bubbles as easy as nitrogen. Twice as much oxygen than nitrogen can dissolve in your blood and tissues without reaching saturation. And the fourth reason is simply that there is a lot more nitrogen than oxygen in the air that you breathe.

Key things to remember:

When you come up from a dive the nitrogen in your tissues is in a state of super-saturation. As long as you go up slowly it will do so without forming bubbles. However, if the pressure gradient is too high, bubbles may form in your blood and tissues. The formation of bubble requires 'gas micronuclei'. Nitrogen diffuses into these gas micronuclei and forms tiny micro bubbles. The micro bubbles are so tiny that they flow back to the heart without causing any blockages. We call these bubbles 'silent bubbles' and we can detect them with a Doppler Ultrasound Flow Meter. The more nitrogen is released, the more bubbles grow. So if you go up to quickly or if you stay too long at depth, more nitrogen is trying to leave your tissues and larger bubbles form. When bubbles become larger they block blood flow. Bubbles cause different problems on different places. Type I decompression sickness is when bubbles form in the joints and ligaments, and under the skin (subcutaneous or skin bends). It causes pain only and is not life threatening. Three quarters of decompression sickness cases are type I. Type II decompression sickness is more serious and can be life threatening. In most cases bubbles affect the central nervous system, causing tingling, numbness, loss of bladder control, difficulty with balance and in the worst cases, paralysis. Bubbles can also affect the lungs (pulmonary DCS) causing shortness of breath and coughing (the chokes) or the heart causing low blood pressure and unconsciousness. Rarely, bubbles re-enter the heart from the lungs and are pumped to the rest of the body. Bubbles can also form or end up in the brain (cerebral DCS) causing tunnel vision, dizziness, confusion, and if bubbles block key areas where, for example your heart rate is regulated, it can lead immediately to death. Oxygen does not cause decompression sickness, because it does not have the chance to form bubbles. The risk of decompression sickness is very, very small when you dive within the limits of your table or computer.

Find out more:

http://en.wikipedia.org/wiki/Decompression_sickness

RISK OF DECOMPRESSION SICKNESS

Decompression sickness risks and efficiency of the circulatory system.

Almost all cases of decompression sickness are the result of not following the rules and staying within limits. You have to be extra careful in some cases. All these cases have to do with changes in your circulation and blood. As long as you remember that, you do not have to memorise this list. You can make it up yourself.

1) Age. As you get older everything works less efficiently, and that means that you off-gas nitrogen less efficiently.

2) Poor condition (health and fitness). If you are in good shape you have less chance of getting decompression sickness, because your circulatory system tends to be more efficient.

3) Exercise immediately before, during or immediately after a dive. Exercise before and during a dive can mean that your tissues take on nitrogen more quickly due to your increased heart rate. Exercise before during or after a dive also increases the number of micronuclei in your blood, increasing the chances of bubble formation during off-gassing.

4) Injuries. Blood flow to and from an injury site is reduced increasing the chance that bubbles may form.

5) Large temperature changes before, during and after the dive. Differences in temperature cause changes in circulation and increase the risk of bubble formation.

6) Patent Foramen Ovale (PFO see the section above). Bubbles can more easily get into the arteries through a hole in your heart.

The following are often mentioned, but research is inconclusive or simply does not yet exist:

7) Being overweight. Nitrogen dissolves more easily in fat than in water (blood), meaning that if you have a lot of fat you take on a lot of nitrogen.

8) Being a woman (women on average have more fat and less efficient circulation).

9) Dehydration. If you are dehydrated you blood is thicker blood meaning that your circulation is slower and bubbles are more likely to form.

10) Alcohol. Alcohol causes dehydration. However, existing studies have found no effect.

11) Reverse dive profiles. Many dive operators recommend that you make the deepest dive first, and not to go up and down during a dive. This recommendation is outdated. If you do not go deeper than 40 m, and your depth differences during a dive do not exceed 12 m, there is nothing to worry about.

What should you do if you think someone has decompression sickness but that person is conscious and breathing? Easy, give pure oxygen (if that is not available give them enriched air if possible) and go to a doctor. It may not be necessary to alert EMS, but the victim must go to an medical facility. Of course, it is their own decision, but you should insist that they go to a medical facility. Never, ever assume that everything is all right, stop giving oxygen, and tell them to go home. That is decision is not yours to make, never! If the victim is unconscious, or has trouble breathing, do not wait for someone else to take action, you have to act immediately, otherwise everyone is waiting for everyone else to do something. Check that the victim is breathing and that the heart is beating, and if you can wake up the victim. If this not the case, or all signs are weak, you must alert EMS (emergency medical services) immediately, first thing, or have someone do this. You are going to need medical help as soon as possible. Now, if the diver is breathing strongly enough, the heart is beating as well. You can give oxygen using a demand valve, because this way the oxygen lasts longest. If the diver is breathing weakly supply oxygen with a non-breather mask and continuous flow system, until the EMS arrive. In the worst case, the victim is unconscious, and is not breathing, no heartbeat. This means you have to start CPR (cardiopulmonary resuscitation) immediately. Do not wait until the oxygen is there, start right away. When the oxygen is kit is there, you should go on with giving CPR with oxygenated rescue breaths using the continuous flow system until the EMS arrive (or until the victim is conscious and breathing again of course). Do not be afraid to make mistakes: anything, anything, you do is better than doing nothing. You can see it this way: if you do not do anything, because you are afraid to make mistakes, the victim stays dead. Do something. You really cannot make it worse, can you?

Why give oxygen? Oxygen helps for two reasons: firstly, nitrogen bubbles block blood flow, so we want to enrich the diver's blood with as much oxygen as possible so that some still manages to pass around the bubbles, and, secondly breathing a high level of oxygen means that the partial pressure of the nitrogen in the breathing air is very low, while the nitrogen partial pressure in the pulmonary capillaries is much higher, (this difference is called the pressure gradient, remember), so nitrogen diffuses through the alveoli more quickly. This is of course different from "oxygen pushes nitrogen out", as you might have heard it said before.

Key things to remember:

Some factors can make decompression sickness more likely. Many of them involve changes in circulation. You should be familiar with them and be more conservative in your dive planning if any of them apply to you or a diver you are responsible for. If you suspect that a diver has decompression sickness supply them with 100 percent oxygen and seek medical attention. Breathing 100 percent oxygen helps because it increases the amount of oxygen supplied to the tissues affected by blocked blood flow, and it is also increases the nitrogen pressure gradient in the lungs making nitrogen release more efficient.

Find out more:

http://en.wikipedia.org/wiki/Nitrogen_narcosis
http://en.wikipedia.org/wiki/Medical_ultrasonography
http://en.wikipedia.org/wiki/Decompression_sickness
http://en.wikipedia.org/wiki/Foramen_ovale_(heart)
http://depts.washington.edu/dcistudy/DivingResearch/DCIrisk.html
http://www.si.edu/dive/library_reverseprofiles.htm
http://www.ncbi.nlm.nih.gov/pubmed/16509284

http://www.engineeringtoolbox.com/gases-solubility-water-d_1148.html

BAROTRAUMAS

Barotraumas are injuries caused by pressure (in Greek 'trauma' means 'wound'), or rather, they are caused by changes in the ambient pressure. They can happen on descents or ascents in all body air spaces: your lungs, ears and sinuses.

Lung over-expansion injuries

Arterial gas embolism, pneumothorax,
mediastinal emphysema and subcutaneous emphysema.
Decompression Illness.

Lung expansion injuries can happen when you hold your breath and go up. Remember the balloon we talked about in the passage on pressure and volume in the physics of diving section? You can imagine that if you hold your breath at depth and then go up, as the pressure decreases your lungs will expand in a similar way to the balloon. Now remember how delicate your alveoli are? They are much, much more delicate than the rubber of a balloon, and are damaged easily. This is why you must never hold your breath when diving. This risk is greatest in shallow water, where pressure differences are the greatest. Take a look:

Depth Pressure

0 m 1 Bar

10 m 2 Bar

20 m 3 Bar

From a depth of 0 meters to 10 metres, the pressure goes from 1 Bar to 2 Bar, so the pressure is twice as high. But from a depth of 10 to 20 metres, the pressure goes from 2 Bar to 3 Bar, so is only 1.5 times as high. The closer to the surface you are, the greater is the pressure difference. Going up from a depth of two meters holding your breath with full lungs can cause serious problems. This means that if you are working as a dive professional, and are conducting some sort of Emergency Swimming Ascent exercise in open water, it is very important that you watch closely that your students are not holding their breath.

You can treat decompression injuries and lung overexpansion injuries the same way: monitor heart beat and breathing, supply 100 percent oxygen and alert EMS. Because you don't need to differentiate between the conditions when giving first aid, we have one umbrella term for both of them:

Decompression Illness (DCI). So: Decompression Sickness (DCS) plus lung overexpansion injuries = Decompression Illness (DCI).

Let's have a look at lung over-expansion injuries. There are four types of lung over-expansion injuries (you can see them all in Figure 39):

Arterial Gas Embolism (AGE). This is the most serious type of lung overexpansion injury. An embolism is a piece of material or a bubble that causes a blockage your blood vessels. In this case it is an air bubble that causes a blockage in your arteries. This bubble comes from the lungs, because while going up, the expanding air is forced through the alveoli into the blood vessels that go back to the heart via the pulmonary vein. The heart then pumps bubbles via the aorta to the arteries and the rest of the body. There is a good chance that the air bubbles will travel via the carotid arteries up to your brain. This has serious consequences and can lead to immediate unconsciousness. Unlike decompression sickness, you see the symptoms of AGE straight away after a dive, sometimes even before the diver surfaces.

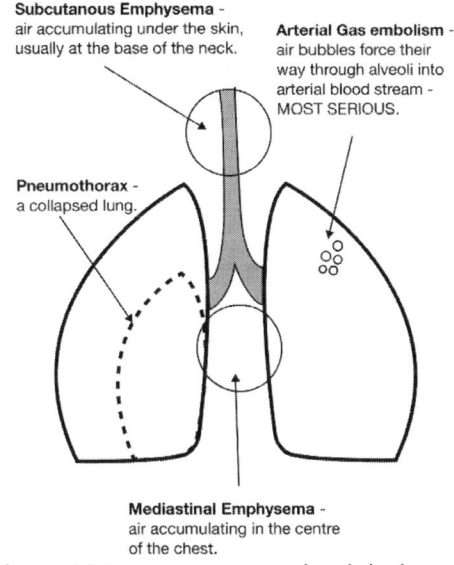

Subcutanous Emphysema - air accumulating under the skin, usually at the base of the neck.

Arterial Gas embolism - air bubbles force their way through alveoli into arterial blood stream - MOST SERIOUS.

Pneumothorax - a collapsed lung.

Mediastinal Emphysema - air accumulating in the centre of the chest.

Figure 39 Lung overexpansion injuries

Pneumothorax or collapsed lung (in Greek 'pneumo-' means lung or air and 'thorax' means chest). Expanding air forces its way between the lung and the chest wall, compressing the lung and causing it to collapse. This is not as dangerous as AGE, because it is unlikely to happen in both lungs, meaning that the victim still has one working lung. But victims suffer from severe chest pain and have difficulty breathing, and they usually cough up blood. Some people have a condition where they can suffer a spontaneous pneumothorax. Of course, people with such a condition cannot ever go diving. Smoking can also harm the protective layer that prevents the side of the lungs from sticking together and this can make pneumothorax more likely. First aid: Try to position the victim on the side of the collapsed lung, although this may hurt. It will be painful, but it will enable the good lung to be used optimally.

Mediastinal emphysema. This is usually comes together with AGE or a pneumothorax. Air leaking from a leak in the lung tissue goes to the centre of the chest. This can restrict the heart, and if the victim did not have pneumothorax, this air may cause pneumothorax as a side effect too. The diver will have severe chest pain, and often difficulty breathing and voice distortion. Subcutaneous emphysema (see below) also happens often at the same time.

Subcutaneous emphysema (in Latin 'sub' means under and 'cutis' means skin). Air leaking from the lung goes under the skin, usually in the neck and chest. You will be able to see swelling in the neck, and the victim may also have chest pain, neck pain and difficulty breathing. Touching the bubbles will make a crackling sound. This is not a very dangerous condition in itself, it is more a sign to keep looking if something more serious is going to happen.

Key things to remember:

There are four types of lung overexpansion injuries: Arterial gas embolism (the most serious), pneumothorax, mediastinal emphysema and subcutaneous emphysema. First aid for decompression sickness and all types of lung overexpansion injuries is the same: monitor the lifeline, supply 100 percent oxygen and alert EMS. Because you don't need to differentiate between the conditions when giving first aid, we have one umbrella term for both of them: decompression illness.

Find out more:

http://en.wikipedia.org/wiki/Air_embolism

http://en.wikipedia.org/wiki/Pneumothorax

http://en.wikipedia.org/wiki/Pneumomediastinum

http://en.wikipedia.org/wiki/Subcutaneous_emphysema

Ear and sinus barotraumas

Outer ear, middle ear and inner ear.
Eustachian Tube and equalisation: Valsalva and Frenzel.
Ruptured eardrum, and reverse blocks.

Your ear has three parts: the outer ear including your ear canal, the middle ear, which is separated from the outer ear by your ear drum, and the inner ear, which is filled with liquid and contains your cochlea, the organ you hear with, and your vestibular canal, the organ that gives you information about your balance. You can see a picture of the ear in Figure 40. All injuries of the ear, the barotraumas, are in the middle ear, because it is the only air space that does not equalise itself. Your outer ear is open to the environment, so the pressure there is always equal to the ambient pressure, and your inner ear is filled with fluid and so not affected by pressure changes.

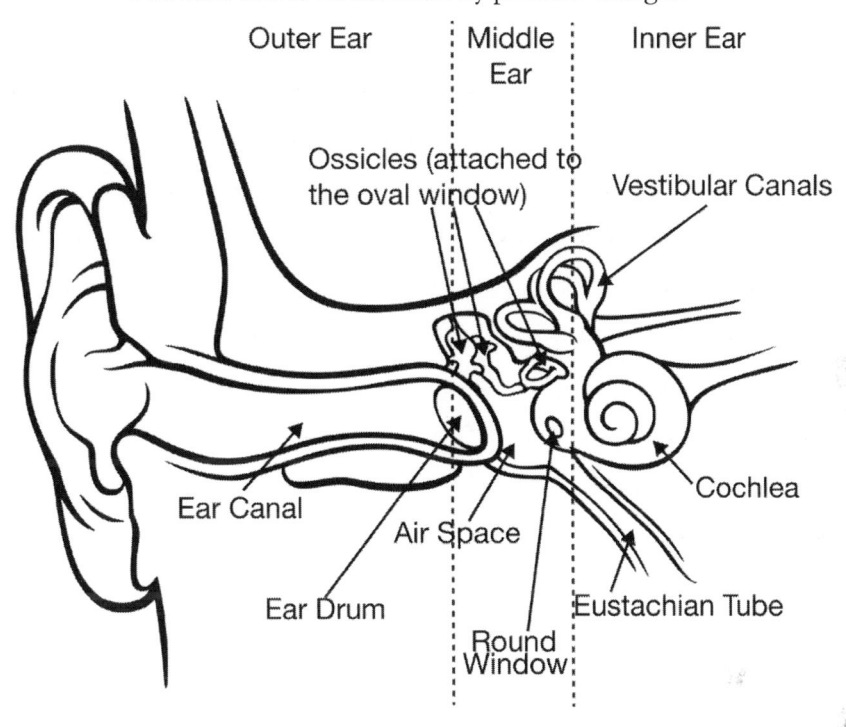

Figure 40 The ear

To keep the pressure in the middle air the same as the pressure outside, air must be able to go in and out of the space. Air is able to do this through the Eustachian Tube, a tube connecting your middle ear with your throat. When you equalise descending on a dive, you push air through the Eustachian tube into the middle ear. The tube is normally closed by a muscle, but this muscle relaxes when you swallow or yawn. When you have a cold or congestion the Eustachian tube is filled with mucus, and this is why you are unable to equalise with a cold.

Some divers can equalise underwater simply by swallowing or yawning, and letting the air just flow in through the open tube. For many divers, especially new divers, this does not work well, because the pressure changes too quickly, particularly in shallow water, and the tube is closes before enough air has gone through. The solution is to push air under pressure through the tube. There is a good way and a bad way to this. The bad way is pinching your nose and breathing against it: the Valsalva manoeuvre (named after Antonio Maria Valsalva, a 17th-century physician and anatomist from Bologna who described the use of this manoeuvre to push out pus). This is not the best way because you can build up too much pressure, and you damage the round window. The round window is a moveable membrane in your ear that sits against your cochlea, and can go back and forth to compensate for pressure changes. A ruptured round window is a serious problem that can cause permanent hearing loss and balance problems. Teach your students to exhale most of their breath before equalising with the Valsalva manoeuvre, so not too much pressure is placed on the round window. Better still, teach them the Frenzel manoeuvre, named after Herman Frenzel, a German ear, nose and throat physician and Luftwaffe commander, who developed this for bomber pilots). In a Frenzel, you push the air through the tube with pressure built up from moving your tongue up and to the back, instead of using the enormous pressure of your chest muscles as in the Valsalva. Practically all experienced divers use the Frenzel method, although they sometime think it is called a Valsalva.

If you don't equalise or equalise too late you can rupture your eardrum. If this happens you will feel a pressure build up (a squeeze) followed by a very sharp pain. When the eardrum breaks, water enters your middle ear, and this comes into contact with your vestibular canals - the balance organ. This will cause vertigo and nausea. This is not very serious, because your eardrum will repair itself, but you have to stay out of the water while it does so, because water in your middle ear can cause dangerous infections. A visit to a physician is necessary. In less severe cases, a severe squeeze can cause your middle ear and cavities to fill with blood and other fluids, which is another way your body tries to equalise if you do not it yourself with air. There is no pain straight after the dive, but you will have a full feeling in your ear, as if there is still water in it. That is of course the remaining fluid. It will go away by itself, but if there is continuing pain, you should see a doctor or get you student to see one.

Usually when you equalise your ears, you also equalise your sinuses, unless there is any congestion. If you have congestion in your sinuses you will feel pain around your eyebrows and to either side of your nose above your teeth. If you descend slowly, you might be able to equalise past the congestion, but you can have the same problem on ascent (when you have no choice but to go up) so it can be better to end the dive. A sinus squeeze can cause a nosebleed, it is not usually serious, but it can be painful.

When going up from a dive you don't normally have to do anything, the air you added on the descent escapes easily. However if the Eustachian tube is blocked, air cannot escape. This is called a reverse block. This happens when you have a cold or congestion and are using decongestants that wear off during the dive, or if blow your nose heavily before you descend but mucus builds up again during the dive. Unfortunately, you have no choice, you have to go up when you run out of air (descends are optional, ascends are not!). The only thing you can do is go up very slowly. If the air still cannot escape you will have to rupture your eardrum. This is why it is not a good idea to dive with a cold or congestion, and why it is also a good idea to go up with at least 50 bar in your tank, so you have some time to solve problems like this.

Key things to remember:

Your ear consists of your outer ear, middle ear and inner ear. Only your middle ear is affected by changes in pressure because it is an airspace, your outer ear is open to the environment and your inner ear is liquid filled. Your Eustachian tube connects your throat to your middle ear, allowing you to add air to your middle ear as you descend by equalising with the Valsalva manoeuvre(lungs) or the Frenzel manoeuvre (tongue). If you delay equalisation and attempt a forceful Valsalva manoeuvre you can rupture your round window. If you fail to equalise, you will rupture your ear drum. You will feel an increase in pressure (a squeeze) followed by a sharp pain. You will then suffer from vertigo and nausea because water enters your middle ear and comes into contact with your vestibular canals. If you dive with a cold or congestion you can suffer from a reverse block: the air cannot escape from the middle ear through the Eustachian tube because it is blocked.

Find out more:

http://en.wikipedia.org/wiki/Ear
http://en.wikipedia.org/wiki/Ear_clearing
http://en.wikipedia.org/wiki/Decongestant

TEMPERATURE PROBLEMS

Hyperthermia: heat exhaustion and heat stroke.
Vasodilatation and vasoconstriction.
Hypothermia.

Normal body temperature at rest is usually 37°C. If you get too hot, you can suffer from hyperthermia, heat exhaustion followed by heat stroke, and if you get too cold you can suffer from hypothermia (there you have hyper- and hypo- again).

When you get hot, your body responds by relaxing and widening the blood vessels in your skin. This is called vasodilatation, and this increases heat loss by letting more blood flow to the skin allowing the heat escape. This is why you get red when you are hot. You also sweat, which evaporates and speeds up heat loss. If this still does not reduce your body temperature sufficiently, you will sweat more and your heart rate will get higher. Because your blood vessels are dilated (so wider than usual) pressure in the circulatory system is low, causing your heart beat to be faster but weaker (weaker, because there is not much tension on your blood vessels). You can detect this as a rapid but weak pulse rate. This stage of overheating is called heat exhaustion. You can relieve these symptoms by moving the victim to a cool shaded area and getting them to drink water. You can even wrap them in a damp towel to speed cooling. You do not have to go to a doctor if they recover quickly.

If a victim suffering from heat exhaustion continues to heat, all cooling mechanisms will fail and the body gives up. There is no more sweating, so the skin will be hot and dry to the touch. The blood vessels under your skin are no longer dilated, so there is a rapid and strong pulse. This is highly dangerous and life threatening because your internal organs, including your brain, begin to overheat. This stage of overheating is called heat stroke. If you suspect heat stroke, alert EMS immediately, and try to cool the victim as much as you can: get them out of the Sun and surround them with wet towels, and encourage them to drink water. Never put them in ice because this can cool them too quickly and cause a heart attack. Monitor the lifeline while you wait for EMS to arrive.

When you get too cold instead of too hot, your body responds in exactly the opposite way to when as to when you are hot: the blood vessels in your skin constrict (vasoconstriction) and your heart rate slows to restrict heat loss. You will also start to shiver to produce muscle heat. If this continues you will become tired, your breathing will be fast and you will shiver continuously. You will feel numbness in your extremities as your body increases vasoconstriction to conserve heat for your organs. These are the signs of mild hypothermia. If you start to shiver continuously on a dive, don't delay, end the dive immediately and seek warmth. (Oh, and by the way, you will be told over and over again that you lose a lot of body heat from your head. This is complete nonsense, of course. Your head has less than 10% of the body's total surface area. To lose 'most body heat' it would have to lose about 40 times as much heat per as every other part of your body. That is not happening of course, and tests show that we lose the same amount of heat whatever the exposed skin. Have fun arguing).

Moderate hypothermia sets in when the body temperature lowers to between 32°C and 28°C. Signs and symptoms include loss of coordination, confusion, loss of attention span and judgement, slurred speech and shallow breathing. Someone suffering from moderate hypothermia should seek immediate medical attention. If necessary alert EMS, or take them to the nearest emergency medical facility. Try to insulate them as much as possible.

When body temperature drops below 28°C your body's heat conserving mechanisms will fail. When your body progresses from a state of moderate hypothermia to advanced hypothermia, you will initially feel warm because vasoconstriction stops and blood rushes back to your skin and your extremities. You will also stop shivering. This is extremely dangerous because you now lose heat at an uncontrolled rate, which quickly leads to unconsciousness, slowing of the heart and death. Someone in a severe hypothermic state may appear to be dead, but with proper medical care they can sometimes be resuscitated, so it is important to get them to emergency medical care as soon as possible.

Key things to remember:

Your body responds to hyperthermia with vasodilatation and sweating. Due to vasodilatation your pulse will be rapid but weak. This is called heat exhaustion. If you continue to overheat and your body temperature exceeds 40°C, your body's cooling mechanisms can stop working. You will stop sweating so your skin will be hot and dry to the touch, and vasodilatation will stop, meaning that your pulse will now be rapid and strong. This is called heat stroke. Heat stroke is life threatening and requires immediate medical attention. Your body responds to hypothermia with vasoconstriction and shivering. Moderate hypothermia sets in when the body temperature lowers to between 32°C and 28°C Signs and symptoms include loss of coordination, confusion, loss of attention span and judgement, slurred speech and shallow breathing. If body temperature drops below 28°C you progress from a state of moderate hypothermia to advanced hypothermia. You will initially feel warm because your body's heat conserving mechanisms fail: vasoconstriction stops and blood rushes back to your skin and your extremities. You will also stop shivering. This is extremely dangerous because you now lose heat at an uncontrolled rate, which quickly leads unconsciousness, slowing of the heart rate and death.

Find out more:

http://en.wikipedia.org/wiki/Heat_illness
http://en.wikipedia.org/wiki/Hypothermia
http://www.webmd.com/a-to-z-guides/features/do-we-really-lose-most-of-our-heat-through-our-heads

DECOMPRESSION THEORY

Enough about what can go wrong. We will now look how we can avoid problems: how do we know how long, how deep and how often you can dive safely? All of you have used dive tables and dive computers. It's good to know how these things work. But how did we develop these dive tables and decompression models and how do we know they work? After all, you trust your life to them. In this chapter, you will learn that decompression models use half-times, compartments (theoretical tissues) and M-values, and better still, you will understand what these are.

HALF-TIMES

Exponential nitrogen filling of tissues: half times.
Fast and slow tissues.

During a dive, nitrogen dissolves into your all your body tissues, but some tissues uptake nitrogen faster than other tissues. As a rule of thumb, tissues and organs that receive a lot of blood, such as your brain, uptake nitrogen quickly and release it quickly. Tissues that have a lower blood flow, such as bone, uptake nitrogen very slowly, and release it very slowly. Besides blood flow, the density of tissue is also an important factor in nitrogen uptake: nitrogen cannot enter dense, impenetrable tissues like bone as easy as open tissues like your liver or kidneys. The other very important factor in how quickly a tissue uptakes nitrogen, is how much nitrogen is already dissolved in the tissue. The more nitrogen already in a tissue, the harder it is to get more nitrogen in. Another way to say this: the smaller the nitrogen pressure gradient between the tissue and the blood, the slower nitrogen will dissolve into the tissue. It is the same when you fill a scuba tank: when the tank is empty the air goes in faster than when the tank is half full. Initially when the partial pressure of nitrogen in the blood in much higher than that of the tissue, nitrogen will dissolve more quickly. But the more nitrogen that dissolves into the tissue, the smaller difference of the nitrogen partial pressure between the blood and tissue will be, and so the rate at which nitrogen dissolves will slow down. A tissue does not fill with a constant rate, like water filling a glass, but exponentially: slower and slower while the tissue gets fuller, like blowing up a balloon.

That makes it a bit hard to calculate how much nitrogen is in a tissue. With a glass of water it is easy: simple, how much water per second goes in, times how many seconds you fill it up. But with body tissues and nitrogen the rate at which nitrogen goes in changes all the time. Fortunately, there is a simple trick. This trick is to use half-times. (And yes, that is same trick as physicists use for nuclear reactions, for instance). A half-time of a body tissue is the amount of time it takes to fill half of the remaining space. If the tissue is empty, after one half-time the tissue will be half full. Now that the tissue is half full, there is only half of the tissue left to fill, so over the next half-time, nitrogen will fill up a quarter of the total space, and the tissue will now be three-quarters full. So, after two half times a tissue is not full, it is only half, plus half of the remaining half full. And so on: now that the tissue is three-quarters full, there is only a quarter of the total space left to fill, so over the next half-time, nitrogen will fill up one-eighth of the total space, and the tissue will now be seven-eighths full. You can see, with this trick you compensate for the fact that nitrogen goes slower and slower into the tissue when the tissue has absorbed more and more nitrogen. Let us have one more at this, but now using percentages, that is easier:

1 half-time - 50%
2 half-times - 50% + 25% = 75%
3 half-times - 75% + 12.5% = 87.5%
4 half-times - 87.5% + 6.2% = 93.8%
5 half-times - 93.8% + 3.1% = 96.9%
6 half-times - 96.9% + 1.5% = 98.4%

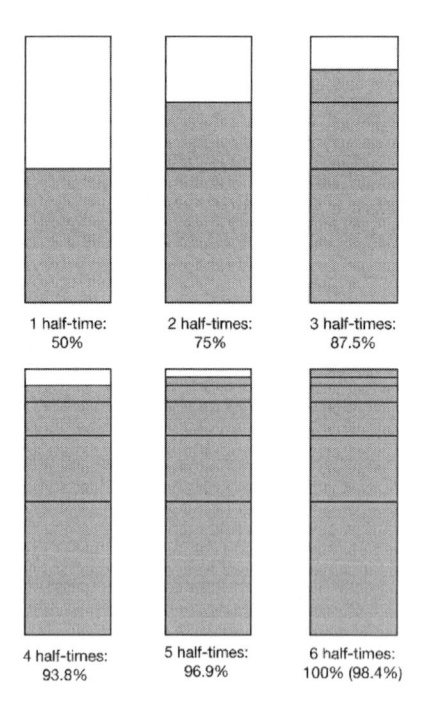

Figure 41 Half times

You can see in Figure 41 that less and less nitrogen dissolves in each half-time. You can also see that you would never reach 100 percent! Look at the percentages after six half times: they are so small, that it is OK t say that a tissue is full (or empty) after six half times. Now, remember that some tissues like muscles absorb and release nitrogen quickly, while some tissues like bone absorb and release nitrogen slowly. We call these fast tissues and slow tissues (surprise!). How do say this using half times? Well, fast tissues fill up fast, so they have low half times, while slow tissues fill up slowly, so they have long half times. For example, a fast tissue with a half-time of five minutes will already be half full after five minutes, and it will be full after six half time - six times five equals thirty minutes. But it will take slow tissue with a half-time of sixty minutes 60 minutes to be half full, and no less than 360 minutes (60 minutes x 6 half-times = 360 minutes) to be full of nitrogen. See the difference? It is just a trick, but a good trick.

Key things to remember:

Different body tissues fill up at different rates with nitrogen during a dive. This filling up goes slower and slower when the tissues get fuller and fuller. We use half times to express this. 1 half-time - 50% full, 2 half-times - 50% + 25% = 75% full , 3 half-times - 75% + 0.125% = 87.5% full , 4 half-times - 87.5% + 6.2% = 93.8% full, 5 half-times - 93.8% + 3.1% = 96.9% full, 6 half-times - 96.9% + 1.5% = 98.4% full. We say a tissue is full after 6 half times. Tissues that fill up fast have low half times, tissues that fill up slowly have high half times.

Find out more:

http://en.wikipedia.org/wiki/Half_time_(physics)

COMPARTMENTS (THEORETICAL TISSUES)

Compartments and theoretical tissues.
Different decompression models.
The nitrogen loading of a compartment in pressure in metres of seawater.

The first decompression model and dive tables were developed in 1906 by the Scottish physiologist John Scott Haldane, and all our modern decompression models are still based on Haldane's original model. He was the guy who came up with the idea of using the half time trick in diving to allow for slow and fast tissues. But how do we make a model out of that? There are hundreds or thousands of tissues in your body, and we cannot measure the precise half time for each and every one of those. This would be way too much of work and it would not be practical either, because different rates in different tissues would vary from person to person, so you would have to measure a lot of people and take averages, and the Figures would be just that, averages.

So we need another trick. Haldane reasoned like this: who cares about the half time of real tissues? We can just make a model with as many "theoretical tissues" with different half time as we like, and see of it works or not. Use a model of six tissues with mostly long half times, or 12 tissues with high and low half time, or use only two tissues: whatever you want, as long as it works! The theoretic tissues in a decompression model do not represent a real tissue in the human body, it is simply a mathematical model that has been shown to work. But how do you know if it works or not? Experiments: calculate with a model, put someone in a decompression chamber and see if they get ill or not! Haldane was famous for testing models on himself and his family and friends, often making them quite sick. But mainly he experimented with goats in a decompression chamber, before refining his data with human volunteers. Well, not really volunteers, but soldiers who just had to do what they were told. This means his volunteers didn't represent a diverse population, and his models were not suited to people of all genders, ages, and bodily features, but at that stage it didn't really matter because only fit military men were divers. When the PADI RDP was developed in the 1980s, there were two big improvements: 1) all sorts of people with regard to age and body type were used in the test. 2) We did not have to go as far as making the actually sick, because we can use an ultra-sound device to look inside the body at bubble formation before anything happens. Modern models are very refined and very safe because of this.

So let's go back to the model: how many tissues and with what half time did work? We found no evidence that using hundreds of half-time rates is better than using just a few, in fact, using a lot of them it makes it harder to work with. This is good news, of course. Let's look at a few examples of the number theoretical tissues used by different models: Haldane's original decompression model used five different tissue half-times, the US Navy tables use six, the PADI RDP uses fourteen, and the Suunto algorithm uses nine. This means you cannot interchange pressure groups between different tables, i.e. between the US Navy tables and the PADI RDP, because on different tables the pressure group designations represent different theoretical levels of nitrogen. For example an F pressure group on the US Navy tables represents a different level of nitrogen than an F pressure group on the PADI RDP.

Theoretical tissues are usually called compartments: a theoretical tissue and a compartment are exactly the same thing. So, a decompression model is a calculation trick that uses a certain number of compartments with different half time. Let's look a bit closer, and do some simple calculations.

When a dive is deeper, the pressure is high, and more nitrogen dissolves into all tissues. The higher the pressure, the more atoms you can get into the tissue, just like in your tank. This means that a tissue that is half full at 10 metres contains less nitrogen than the same tissue that is half full at 20 meters. And this means it is not enough to say: tissue A is half full. How much nitrogen there is in a 'half-full' tissue, depends on the ambient pressure (the depth).

. To make things easy, we talk about the amount of nitrogen in a compartment in metres of seawater. At 10 metres, a compartment that is half full, will have half of the pressure of 10 metres of seawater: 5 metres of seawater. And at 20 metres, the same compartment that is again 50 percent full will now have half of twenty metres, so 10 metres of pressure. Nice: we do not even have to calculate the pressure at that depth, we just use the depth itself. So, to know the nitrogen pressure in a compartment you simple look how full it is and you multiply it by the depth! Have look at the table for an example that brings it all together.

Time	How full	Depth		
		10m	20m	30m
1 half-time	50%	50% x 10 = 5msw	50% x 20 = 10msw	50% x 30 = 15msw
2 half-times	50% + 25% = 75%	75% x 10 = 7,5msw	75% x 20 = 15 msw	75% x 30 = 22,5msw

Let's look at the table and do some dives. We have:

1) A compartment with a half time of 10 minutes

2) A dive of 20 metres

3) 20 minutes at that depth.

First let us look at the number of half times, as we did in the second column of the table. For a compartment with a 10 minute half-time, twenty minutes is two half-times (2 x 10 minutes), and after two half-times a compartment is 75 percent full (first half-time 50% + second half-time 25% = 75% in total).

Second: We can work out how many metres of seawater of pressure there is in the compartment, like in the third, fourth and fifth column of the table:

75% of 20 metres is 15 metres (20 metres x 0.75 = 15 metres), therefore the compartment has 15 metres of seawater nitrogen pressure. See Figure 42. And that is all. The only thing we now have to decide is: how much pressure in metres of seawater is still safe? We need to use maximum values, M-values. How? By experiments again.

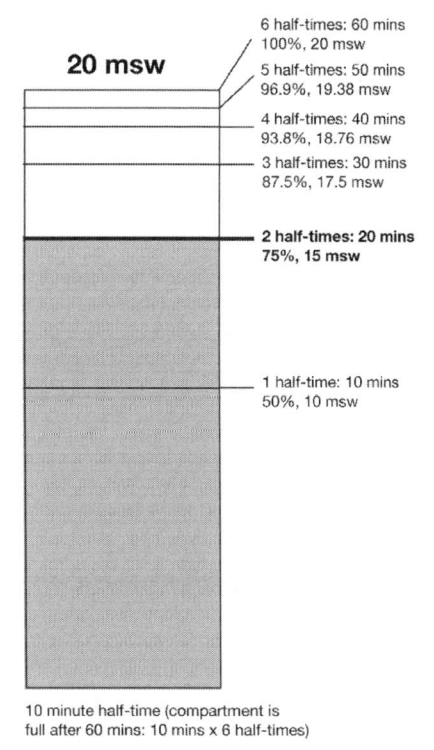

Figure 42 Compartments and pressure in msw

Key things to remember:

Compartments are theoretical tissues with different half times. Decompression models use different numbers of compartments with different half times. The US Navy tables use six, the PADI RDP uses fourteen, and the Suunto algorithm uses nine. This means you cannot interchange pressure groups between different tables. The nitrogen loading of a compartment is expressed by pressure in metres of seawater. You can calculate the nitrogen loading of a compartment by calculating how full it is after a given number of half times in percentages, and multiply this percentage by the depth in metres of sea water.

Find out more:

http://en.wikipedia.org/wiki/Decompression_theory

M-VALUES

M-values as maximum nitrogen loading of compartments.
Different models use different M-values.
Computer models use conservative M-values, Bühlmann M-values, Fast compartments and high M-values,
slow compartments and low M-values.
The controlling compartment.

The M-value is the amount of nitrogen that can be dissolved in a compartment (upon surfacing from a dive) without causing an unacceptable risk of decompression sickness. It is a maximum acceptable pressure in the compartment, and we express the M-value also in metres of seawater. It is M-values that provide maximum dive times in decompression models. In recreational diving when the first compartment nears the M-value you must end the dive. Some tissues can deal with higher levels of nitrogen than others. Fast tissues are tissues where nitrogen goes in fast, and it comes out fast as well. They have small half-times (that is why they are fast). In and out fast means that there is not much time to cause problems, so fast tissues with a small half time can handle high pressures of nitrogen. They have a high maximum value, high M-values. The same goes for slow compartments: slow tissues are tissues where nitrogen goes in slowly, and it comes out slowly as well. They have high half-times (that is why they are slow). In and out slowly means that there is a lot of time to cause problems, so slow tissues with a high half time can handle only low pressures of nitrogen. They have a low maximum value, low M-values.

Fast tissue = low half time = high M-value

Slow tissue = high half time = low M-value

When the first compartment nears the M-value you must end the dive. That is why we call that compartment the controlling compartment. The controlling compartment is not always the same, it is a different compartment depending on how deep you go. This is because of the different M-values of slow and fast compartments. Let me explain:

On deep dives, faster compartments reach their limit the quickest because their half-time rates are the fastest and the pressure is high. Their half time go so fast that they fill up quickly. They have high M-values, but because they fill quickly and because you are deep, you quickly reach these M-values. So, your dive time is short. The slow compartments however fill up slowly. They probably did not even reach the first half time when the quickest compartment is full. So, a deep dive is controlled by fast compartments. And because if this the dive time is short.

However on shallow dives, there is not enough pressure for the fast compartments to reach their high M-values. Their high M-values are higher than the pressure at the depth of the dive, so you will never reach them. So, although the pressure in faster compartments may reach the surrounding pressure the quickest, they cannot reach their M-values, and so cannot control the dive. The slower compartments now control the dive because they can reach their M-values, but do so at a slower rate, meaning that our dive time is longer. Shallow dives are controlled by slow compartments.

An example with numbers see Figure 43:

We have a fast compartment with a half time of 10 minutes and a high M-value of 25msw

We have a slow compartment with a half time of 60 minutes and a low M-value of 5 msw

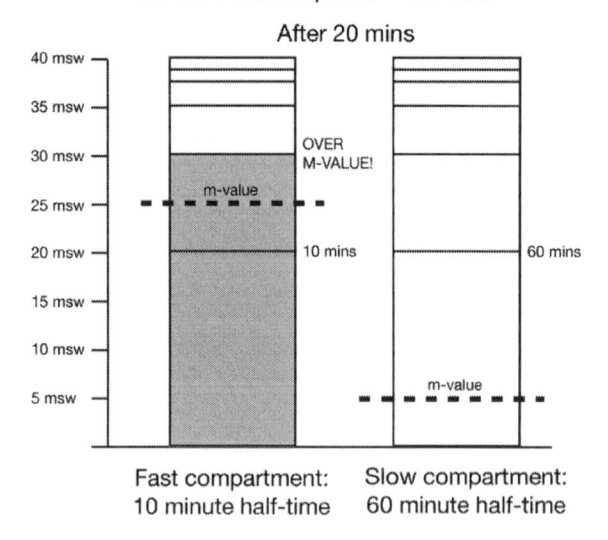

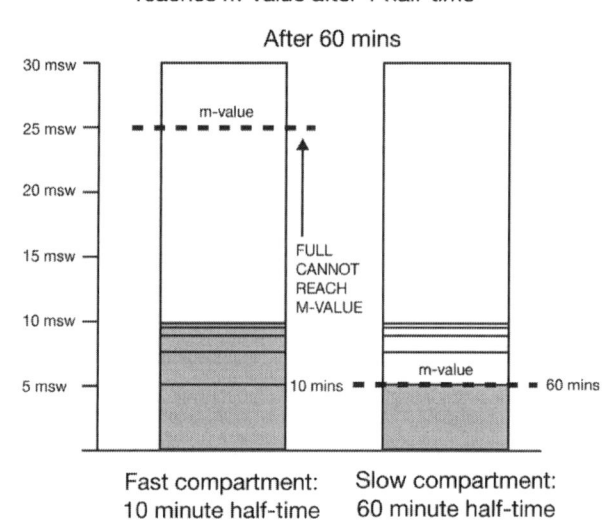

Figure 43 Slow and fast compartments, and M-values

Deep Dive: a short deep dive to 40 m for 20 minutes

Fast compartment: 20 minutes is two half times, 75% full, so the pressure is 75% of 40msw = 30 msw.

That is way over the M-value already!

Slow compartment: 20 minutes is one third half time, so it is basically empty. It did not reach the M-value by far.

So: the fast compartment controls the deep dive.

Shallow Dive: a shallow long dive to 10 metres for 60 minutes

Fast compartment: 60 minutes is 6 half times, so it is full: the pressure =100% 10 msw = 10 msw.

It does not even come near the M-value of 25 msw

Slow compartment: 60 minutes is one half time: 50% 10 msw = 5msw.

It reached the M-value of 5 msw!

So: the slow compartment controls the shallow dive.

M-values are different for different decompression models, such as the RDP, US navy etc. For example, the M-values of the PADI RDP are lower than those the US Navy tables. Dive computer models usually have more conservative, lower M-values than dive tables, often called Bühlmann M-values. If you plan a dive with a computer and with a table, the computer gives you less dive time. But usually the actual dive you make using a computer can be longer! This is because they can calculate dive profiles as they really are, while dive tables have to assume that you spend all of your dive time at your maximum depth. Dive computers write a custom profile on the fly as you are diving, and so they can have lower M-values while allowing you the same or longer dive times as a table does. It eliminates the rounding of depths that you have to do when using dive tables.

Key things to remember:

M-values are the maximum nitrogen loading of compartments. They are determined by experiments detecting of silent bubbles with Doppler Ultra Sound in volunteers. Different models like the PADI RDP, US Navy tables or computer models use different M-values. Computer models usually use more conservative M-values, Bühlmann M-values, because they make dive profiles on the fly and because of this still can give you long dive times. Fast compartments (compartments with small half times) have high M-values, slow compartments (compartments with large half times) have low M-values. The compartment that reaches first reaches its M-value during a dive is the controlling compartment of that dive. It controls when you have to go up. Deep dives are controlled by fast compartments (high M values, small half times), shallow dives are controlled by slow compartments (low M-values, large half times).

REPETITIVE DIVES

The surface interval.
EE washout models.

When you surface from a dive, there is still some nitrogen in your body tissues, and it will take a while to get rid of it. When you make a second dive you still have this residual nitrogen from the previous dive in your body, so you cannot dive as long or as deep as the first dive. We call a dive where you still have residual nitrogen from an earlier dive a repetitive dive A decompression model must be able to tell you how to stay safe on your repetitive dives too! Fortunately, you can use the same model with the same compartments, half times and M-values to calculate how quickly you off-gas (or wash-out) at the surface after a dive.

The US Navy tables and the PADI RDP both choose to use only one compartment to calculate the release of nitrogen during the surface interval. Of course, to be safe, they chose a slow compartment with a high half time. The US Navy tables use the half-time of slowest compartment, which is 120 minutes. The PADI RDP uses 60 minutes compartment. (Ever wondered why the PADI RDP considers a dive made more than a 6 hours after a previous dive to be a non-repetitive dive? 60 minute half-time x 6 half-times = 6 hours, so therefore your body is theoretically free of additional nitrogen.) There is a good reason for this difference: the US navy tables were made for military divers making long single compression dives, and so they use the most conservative compartment; whereas the PADI RDP was made only for recreational no-decompression diving, and so the 120 minute half-time washout rate is an unnecessarily conservative. Test data proves that the 60 minute compartment is safe enough for the no-decompression dives made with the RDP. This means you can make your second and third dive sooner after each other when you use the RDP than if you use the US navy tables.

Dive computers can do even better. They do not have to choose one compartment to calculate the wash out at the surface. These models say that all compartments off gas at the surface at the same rate as they filled up underwater (an exponential uptake, exponential release model', EE washout model). You can see this more easily like this: the compartment that reached its M-value first during the dive, is the one that is used to calculate the surface interval. And because the fast compartments that control deep dives washout quickly at their underwater half-time rate, computers can allow you to make consecutive deep dives with very short surface intervals! Sometimes too short to be really sure. So when you put your computer on, don't turn your brain off: allow an extended surface interval of at least one hour after a deep dive.

Key things to remember:

The US Navy tables use the slowest compartment with a 120 minute half-time as the basis for surface interval nitrogen washout, whereas the PADI RDP uses a compartment with a 60 minute half-time rate. This means that the PADI RDP allows you more time on repetitive dives. Many computer algorithms use EE washout, where the controlling compartment of the dive is used to calculate the following surface interval. This may lead to unacceptable short surface intervals after deep dives.

Find out more:

http://en.wikipedia.org/wiki/Decompression_theory

APPENDIX 1 SUMMARY

THE DIVE ENVIRONMENT

The pull of gravitational fields of the Moon and the Sun creates tides. Although the Sun is larger, the Moon is much closer and has a larger effect. Because of the influence of land formations and the rotation of Earth, there are three different types of tidal patterns in different places on Earth: semi-diurnal (two high tides and two low tides of equal heights per day), diurnal (one high tide and one low tide per day) and mixed tides (two high tides and two low tides of unequal heights per day). At full Moon and new Moon the pull of the gravitational fields is strongest and we call this spring tide. Currents are strongest in the water at this time and conditions for diving are less favourable. At half-Moon the gravitational fields of the Moon and Sun work against each other and we call this neap tide. Currents are generally weakest around this time, meaning that the conditions for diving tend to be better.

There are three causes of currents in the sea: 1) currents caused by tides 2) currents caused by global wind patterns 3) currents caused by upwellings. Currents caused by global wind patterns go clockwise in the Northern Hemisphere and counter-clockwise in the Southern Hemisphere. This is due to the rotation of Earth and it is an example of the Coriolis Effect.

A primary coast is one formed by processes of the land, and a secondary coast is one formed by processes of the sea. The type of coast will have a big effect on the type of diving in the area.

Waves have: 1) the wave height - from crest to trough; 2) the wavelength – distance between two crests; 3) the wave frequency – number of crests per second; 4) the wave propagation (direction); 5) the wave speed. Tsunamis are not caused by the wind, they are caused by underwater Earthquakes, volcanic eruptions and landslides. They are sometimes called tidal waves, but this can be misleading as they are not caused by tides. Five things influence the formation of wind waves: 1) the wind speed; 2) the fetch; 3) the width of the area affected by the fetch; 4) the wind duration; and 5) the water depth. The smallest waves are called ripples or capillary waves (maximum wavelength 2cm). Larger waves are called seas. They separate from their point of origin into swells, whose size is constrained by the wind speed, duration and the fetch. This is a fully developed sea. In shallower water swells slow down, and they become breaking waves when they reach water that is 1.3 times as deep as the height of the wave. They form the surf.

The very bottom of the ocean is called the benthic zone. We call anything above that the pelagic zone. 98% of marine organisms live in the benthic zone. The first 200 metres (approximately) of the ocean where light can reach is called the euphotic zone. From 200 metres to 900-1000 metres where only 1 percent of sunlight reaches is called the disphotic zone. From 1000 metres where no light can reach is called the aphotic zone. The aphotic zone makes up 90 percent of the ocean, but 90 percent of marine organisms live where light can reach. An ecosystem is the system of relationships between organisms living in a particular area and their environment. An ecosystem can be described as a pyramid, but more accurately as a food web. A species is a group of related individual organisms that have the same characteristics or qualities, and who can breed with each other but not members of other species. A population is all of the individuals of a given species in a specific area at a certain time. And a community is all of the populations in a specific area at a certain time. The place in which a species lives is called its habitat. This term can be used to refer to a very large area or small area, dependent on the context in which you are talking. Phytoplankton is the primary producers of the sea and forms the basis of the marine ecosystem. Primary carnivores eat primary producers; secondary carnivores eat primary carnivores and so forth. At each step 90 percent of the energy is lost. Some species benefit from other species without eating each other. We call these types of relationships symbiotic relationships. There are three types of symbiotic relationship: 1) a mutualism, where both organisms benefit from each other; 2) commensalism, where only one organism actually benefits from the relationship, but the other organism is not harmed; 3) parasitism, where one organism benefits from the relationship, and in doing so harms the other organism.

Physics

The three ways in which heat energy is transferred are conduction, convection, radiation. Water conducts heat than twenty times faster than air. We lose body heat underwater mainly through conduction. This heat loss is speeded up by convection. Heat loss through radiation does not affect us.

Sound travels four times faster underwater than at the surface. You can hear sounds from farther away underwater, but you are unable to tell which direction a sound is coming from. You can however hear intensity changes (loud, soft) caused by the distance.

Water is denser than air, and so it weighs more and exerts more pressure than air. Because seawater weighs more than freshwater, at a given depth there is more pressure in seawater than in fresh water. In seawater there is an increase of 1 Bar of pressure every 10 metres, whereas in freshwater the pressure increases by 1 Bar every 10.3 metres. Ambient and absolute pressure mean the same thing: the total pressure of the water and air pressure at the surface. Gauge pressure is only the water pressure: ambient pressure minus one Bar.

If the pressure goes up, the volume goes the same amount down, and the density goes up by the same amount. This is called Boyle's Law. To work out the new volume of a balloon when taking it from the surface to a specific depth, divide the original volume by the pressure at the depth to which you are descending. To work out the new volume of a balloon when taking it from a specific depth to the surface, multiply the original volume by the pressure at the depth from which you are going up. To work out how much air a diver will breathe per minute at a given depth, bring him to the surface, multiply this surface air consumption rate (Bar per min) by the pressure at the new depth

The partial pressure of a gas is the percentage of the pressure caused by that specific gas in a mix of gases. It is the percentage of the gas in the mix multiplied with the pressure of the mix. 21 percent of air is oxygen and 79 percent is nitrogen. At sea level the total pressure of air is 1 Bar. The partial pressure of nitrogen is 0.79 Bar (PP N_2) and the partial pressure of oxygen is 0.21 Bar (PP O_2). Oxygen can become toxic at 56 metres when breathing normal air, but at shallower depths when breathing enriched air Nitrox. Also, carbon monoxide is very dangerous under high partial pressure.

When we heat the gas in a flexible container the volume will go up, and the volume will decrease as the gas cools down. When we heat the gas in an inflexible container the pressure will go up, and pressure will go down as the gas cools. For every 1°C temperature change, the pressure will increase or decrease by 0.6 Bar.

In a saturated liquid, the pressure of the gas dissolved in the liquid is the same as the pressure of the gas in contact with the liquid. In a supersaturated liquid, the pressure of the gas dissolved in the liquid is less than pressure of the gas in contact with the liquid. But the difference in pressure is not too big, and the gas slowly comes out of solution without forming bubbles. In an excessively supersaturated liquid, the pressure of the gas dissolved in the liquid is less than pressure of the gas in contact with the liquid. The difference in pressure is so great that the gas comes out of solution too quickly and forms bubbles.

If the weight of the object is more than the weight of the water it displaces, the object will sink. We call this negative buoyancy. If the weight of the object is less than the weight of the water it displaces, the object will float. We call this positive buoyancy. If the weight of the object is the same as the weight of the water it displaces, the object will neither float nor sink. We call this neutral buoyancy. Because of the salt particles dissolved in seawater, it is heavier than freshwater. Seawater has more force with which to push or buoy an object up; objects are more buoyant in saltwater than in freshwater. We can work out the buoyancy of an object (by how much it floats or sinks) if we know three things: how much the object weighs, the volume of the water the object displaces, and the weight per litre of the water (the constant). Seawater weighs 1.03 kg per litre and freshwater weighs 1 kg per litre. To work out the buoyancy of an object, first find out the weight of the water the object displaces. Then find out the difference between the weight of the object and the weight of the water it displaces. If the object is positively buoyant, the difference in weight is how much weight you would need to add to the object to make it neutrally buoyant. Or if the object is negatively buoyant, you can then see how many litres of air you would need to add to a lift bag to make it neutrally buoyant, by dividing the difference in weight by the weight per litre of the water, either fresh water (1 kilogram per litre) or sea water (1.03 kilogram per litre).

EQUIPMENT

Tanks are made from steel (3AA) or aluminium (3AL). Steel is stronger and has a higher working pressure. Aluminium is more buoyant and less rusty. Tanks have a safety valve called a burst disk, that opens at 140% of the working pressure. Once a year, a tanks needs a visual inspection, where the tank is checked for rust and the O-ring between the tank and the valve that stops rusting caused by galvanic action lubricated or replaced. Depending on local regulations, a hydrostatic test is required every three to seven years. The tank is filled with water and pressurised to 160% of the working pressure, and the amount of expansion of the tank walls is measured. If the tank passes the test, it gets a *stamp with the test date and a + if it is ok to fill it 10% higher than the normal working pressure. If not, it is destroyed. Tanks come with a K valve/yoke, a DIN valve, or an old J valve, that has a 50 Bar warning mechanism*

Regulators are closed circuit, semi closed circuit or the most popular: open circuit. The first stage of an open circuit brings the tank pressure down to an intermediate pressure of about 9 Bars above the ambient pressure. They have an environmental seal or not, and they are balanced or not. An environmental seal stops the first stage from getting dirty or freezing up. A balanced regulator maintains the same breathing ease, no matter how high the demand or how low the supply is, an unbalanced regulator does not. The second stage brings the air pressure back to ambient pressure. It is demand valve that is usually constructed to open with the air flow (downstream), but sometimes it open against the air flow (upstream). An upstream valve needs a pilot valve to open up against the air flow. All second stages have Venturi system that helps to open the main valve. It should be off on the surface to prevent free flowing.

Capillary depth gauges are open systems that show depth by showing a change in volume. They show depth relative to the surface pressure: theoretical depths. This makes them suitable for altitude diving. A disadvantage is that they become less accurate at increasing depths. A bourdon tube works on the same principle, but the pressure straightens a tube connected with clogs to a pointer. Bourdon tubes are open, or closed. A transducer determines depth by measuring the strength of an electric current conducted through porcelain in which the resistance increases at depth because of the compression of the tiny air bubbles in it.

PHYSIOLOGY

Every cell in your body needs oxygen for cellular respiration – the process of transferring energy from food to a useable form. Your blood plasma contains red blood cells, that carry oxygen attached to haemoglobin, a substance that binds with oxygen at a high partial pressure (as it is in your lungs), and releases it when the partial pressure is low (as it is in your cells). Carbon dioxide dissolves in the form of a bicarbonate in your blood plasma and is carried away from your cells. Oxygenated blood is bright red, oxygen-poor blood is dark red. Carbon monoxide binds with haemoglobin over 200 times more easily than oxygen, and it does not unbind, meaning that the haemoglobin cannot transport sufficient oxygen to your cells. This can lead to unconsciousness and death. At depth you may not notice the signs and symptoms of carbon monoxide poisoning because of the high partial pressure of oxygen. Give victims of carbon monoxide poisoning pure oxygen.

Your heart pumps blood around your circulatory system to transport oxygen from your lungs to your tissue cells. The right side of the heart receives de-oxygenated blood from your organs and the left side of the heart receives oxygenated blood from your lungs. The right side then pumps blood to your lungs to pick up oxygen and get rid of carbon dioxide, and the left side pumps blood to your tissue cells to deliver oxygen and pick up carbon dioxide. Bright red oxygen-rich blood is transported to your organs via your arteries, which branch into smaller and smaller vessels. Your arteries end in very fine hair-like blood vessels called capillaries, which is where gas exchange of oxygen and carbon dioxide takes place. Dark red oxygen poor blood is then transported back to your heart via your veins. Your heart rate is controlled by your brain, which responds to baroreceptors that detect blood pressure in particular arteries. If the blood pressure is too high the heart rate decreases, and if it is too low the heart rate increases. An overly tight-fitting hood or exposure suit can compress the carotid arteries and jugular veins in the neck. This can trigger the carotid-sinus reflex, which is when the brain falsely detects high blood pressure and slows the heart rate, and blocked jugular venous return, which is a dangerous build-up of oxygen poor blood in the brain. This can lead to unconsciousness and death.

Your trachea branches into two bronchi which lead to each of your lungs. In your lungs your bronchi branch into bronchioles, which end in very small air sacs with thin membranes called alveoli. The pulmonary capillaries are in contact with the alveoli, and this is where the gas exchange of oxygen and carbon dioxide takes place. The first air to enter your lungs when you breathe in is air from your previous exhalation that sits in your dead air space (mouth, throat and trachea), this air is low in oxygen and high in carbon dioxide. We must breathe deeply enough to take in fresh air as well. When we dive or snorkel, the regulator or snorkel increases dead air space, meaning that we should breath more deeply than usual.

Your urge to breath is not triggered by a depletion of oxygen, but by the build-up of carbon dioxide in your blood. The prefix hypo- means too little of something, and the prefix hyper- means too much of something. Hyperventilation means you are breathing too quickly. Hypoventilation on the other hand means that you are breathing too slowly. Hypoxia means that levels of oxygen in your body are too low. Hyperoxia is when levels of oxygen are too high. When levels of carbon dioxide are too low we call that hypocapnia, and when they are too high we call that hypercapnia. There are a few ways in which you can be affected by hypercapnia: by taking shallow breaths due to overexertion or a bad breathing pattern, from skip breathing, from a malfunctioning rebreather, and from taking insufficient breaths between apnea dives. Initial signs and symptoms of hypercapnia are hyperventilation, shortness of breath, tachycardia, headache and excessive sweating; higher levels of carbon dioxide will lead to mental impairment and unconsciousness. If you excessively hyperventilate before an apnea dive you can suffer a shallow water blackout. You suppress the urge to breathe by lowering the level of carbon dioxide in your blood too far, and you stay under water too long. Underwater, the oxygen in your blood plasma is usable because of the high partial pressure, but when you go up the partial pressure of the oxygen falls rapidly, causing you to black out due to hypoxia. Always take a buddy. The mammalian reflex is present in all mammals, though it is much more pronounced in aquatic mammals, and helps to extend breath-hold time in water of below 21°C with the face submerged in the water. It works by slowing the heart rate and vasoconstriction to preserve oxygen, and at greater depths by filling the chest cavity with blood plasma to prevent the lungs being crushed by the pressure.

Breathing oxygen of a partial pressure of higher than 0.5 PPO2 over an extended period of time irritates your lungs, causing a burning sensation in your throat and lungs, and frequent coughing. It is not a problem in recreational diving because dive times are not long enough to cause symptoms. It can be a problem in technical diving. If you breath oxygen at a partial pressure higher than 1.4 – 1.6 Bar it can affect your central nervous system and lead to convulsions. Convulsions underwater are very dangerous because you are unable to keep your regulator in your mouth and you are likely to drown. It can be a problem within recreational diving limits when using Nitrox.

All gases are narcotic above a certain partial pressure, but some are more narcotic then others. Gas narcosis usually begins to affect you at around 30 metres/4 Bar. It can feel like being drunk, resulting in irresponsible behaviour, but it can also make you feel paranoid. The effects of gas narcosis go away immediately when you go up and the pressure decreases.

When you come up from a dive the nitrogen in your tissues is in a state of super-saturation. As long as you go up slowly it will do so without forming bubbles. However, if the pressure gradient is too high, bubbles may form in your blood and tissues. The formation of bubble requires 'gas micronuclei'. Nitrogen diffuses into these gas micronuclei and forms tiny micro bubbles. The micro bubbles are so tiny that they flow back to the heart without causing any blockages. We call these bubbles 'silent bubbles' and we can detect them with a Doppler Ultrasound Flow Meter. The more nitrogen is released, the more bubbles grow. So if you go up to quickly or if you stay too long at depth, more nitrogen is trying to leave your tissues and larger bubbles form. When bubbles become larger they block blood flow. Bubbles cause different problems on different places. Type I decompression sickness is when bubbles form in the joints and ligaments, and under the skin (subcutaneous or skin bends). It causes pain only and is not life threatening. Three quarters of decompression sickness cases are type I. Type II decompression sickness is more serious and can be life threatening. In most cases bubbles affect the central nervous system, causing tingling, numbness, loss of bladder control, difficulty with balance and in the worst cases, paralysis. Bubbles can also affect the lungs (pulmonary DCS) causing shortness of breath and coughing (the chokes) or the heart causing low blood pressure and unconsciousness. Rarely, bubbles re-enter the heart from the lungs and are pumped to the rest of the body. Bubbles can also form or end up in the brain (cerebral DCS) causing tunnel vision, dizziness, confusion, and if bubbles block key areas where, for example your heart rate is regulated, it can lead immediately to death. Oxygen does not cause decompression sickness, because it does not have the chance to form bubbles. The risk of decompression sickness is very, very small when you dive within the limits of your table or computer.

DECOMPRESSION THEORY

Different body tissues fill up at different rates with nitrogen during a dive. This filling up goes slower and slower when the tissues get fuller and fuller. We use half times to express this. 1 half-time - 50% full, 2 half-times - 50% + 25% = 75% full, 3 half-times - 75% + 0.125% = 87.5% full, 4 half-times - 87.5% + 6.2% = 93.8% full, 5 half-times - 93.8% + 3.1% = 96.9% full, 6 half-times - 96.9% + 1.5% = 98.4% full. We say a tissue is full after 6 half times. Tissues that fill up fast have low half times, tissues that fill up slowly have high half times. Compartments are theoretical tissues with different half times. Decompression models use different numbers of compartments with different half times. The US Navy tables use six, the PADI RDP uses fourteen, and the Suunto algorithm uses nine. This means you cannot interchange pressure groups between different tables. The nitrogen loading of a compartment is expressed by pressure in metres of seawater. You can calculate the nitrogen loading of a compartment by calculating how full it is after a given number of half times in percentages, and multiply this percentage by the depth in metres of sea water. M-values are the maximum nitrogen loading of compartments. They are determined by experiments detecting of silent bubbles with Doppler Ultra Sound in volunteers. Different models like the PADI RDP, US Navy tables or computer models use different M-

values. Computer models usually use more conservative M-values, Bühlmann M-values, because they make dive profiles on the fly and because of this still can give you long dive times. Fast compartments (compartments with small half times) have high M-values, slow compartments (compartments with large half times) have low M-values. The compartment that reaches first reaches its M-value during a dive is the controlling compartment of that dive. It controls when you have to go up. Deep dives are controlled by fast compartments (high M values, small half times), shallow dives are controlled by slow compartments (low M-values, large half times).

The US Navy tables use the slowest compartment with a 120 minute half-time rate as the basis for surface interval nitrogen washout, whereas the PADI RDP uses the median compartment with a 60 minute half-time rate. This means that the PADI RDP allows you more time on repetitive dives. Many computer algorithms use EE washout, where the controlling compartment is used to calculate the surface interval. This may lead to unacceptable short surface intervals after deep dives.

APPENDIX 2 EXAM AND ANSWER KEY

The Dive Environment

1 - Does the Sun or the Moon influence the tides most?

A - Sun **B** - Moon

2 - A pattern of two equally high tides and two equally low tides per day is called

A - Diurnal **B** - Semi-diurnal

3 - When the Sun and the Moon are at a right angle from each other it is

A - Neap tide **B** - Spring tide

4 - On the northern hemisphere, gyres go

A - Clockwise **B** - Counter clock wise

5 - The effect that makes gyres bend to the east or west is called

A - The rotation effect **B** - The Coriolis effect

6 - Upwellings are

A - Water coming up because of volcanic activity **B** - Cold water rising to the surface because of the activity of the wind

7 - A secondary coast is

A - The coast behind the first barrier in the sea **B** - A coast made by processes of the sea

8 - Wave length is the distance from

A - Crest to trough **B** - Crest to crest

9 - The smallest waves at sea are called

A - Swells **B** - Ripples

10 - Swells are the biggest waves at sea

A - TRUE **B** - FALSE

11 - When two crests arrive at the same time at the same location we call this

A - Destructive interference **B** - Constructive interference

12 - The fetch determines

A - Maximum wave height **B** - Destructive inference

13 - A wave breaks in the surf when the depth of the water is

A - Twice the length of the wave **B** - 1.3 times the height of the wave

14 - The disphotic zone is

A - The depth where there is no light **B** - The depth where there is some light

15 - The pelagic zone is

A - The dark depth **B** - The open ocean

16 - An anemone is

A - Benthic **B** - Pelagic

17 - A habitat is a

A - A place where a species prefers to live **B** - A habit of a species

18 - The main primary producer of ecosystems in the sea are

A - Seaweeds **B** - Plankton

19 - When two life forms live together, but only one profits from that, while the other is not damaged we call that

A - Commensalism **B** - Parasitism

Physics

1 - Water conduct heat more than…..faster than air does

A - 4 times **B** - 20 times

2 - The most important heat transmission process for divers is

A - Convection **B** - Conduction

3 - Conduction is

A - The transport of heat energy by atoms or molecules bumping into each other **B** - The transport of heat by rising air or water

4 - The disappearing of colour underwater is

A - Diffusion **B** - Absorption

5 - The fact that shadows are not sharp line underwater is a consequence of

A - Absorption **B** - Diffusion

6 - Visual reversion happens

A - In turbid water **B** - In cold water

7 - Sound travels

A - Four times faster underwater **B** - 33% faster underwater

8 - You cannot hear the …of sound underwater

A - Intensity **B** - Direction

9 - What is the gauge pressure in 23 meters of sea water

A - 2.3 bar **B** - 3.3 bar

10 - What is the ambient pressure in 27 meters of fresh water

A - 3.62 bar **B** - 3.7 bar

11 - What is the new volume of a balloon of 12 litres taken down to 16 meters of fresh water?

A - 4.61 litres **B** - 4.71 litres

12 - What is the new volume of an inflexible container of 8 litres at 12 metres seawater?

A - 8 litres **B** - 3.64 litres

13 - A diver uses 3 bar per minute at a depth of 15 meters of fresh water. How much does he use at 25 meters?

A - 4.18 bar per minute **B** - 4.20 bar per minute

14 - The partial pressure of oxygen of normal air at 25 meters of seawater is

A - 0.74 **B** - 0.52

15 - Breathing air with 0.80% of CO at 21 metres of seawater is equivalent to breathing what percentage of CO at the surface?

A - 2.48% **B** - 0.80%

16 - Is it safe to go to 25 meters of seawater with Enriched Air Nitrox 30% Oxygen?

A - Yes **B** - No

17 - A steel scuba tank is filled with air at 220 bar pressure at 21 degrees Celsius, and cools down to 15 degrees. What is the new pressure within the tank?

A - 216.4 bar **B** - 223.6 bar

18 - Bubble are formed in a liquid that is

A - Saturated **B** - Excessively super saturated.

19 - An object that neither nor floats is

A - Neutrally buoyant **B** - Positively buoyant

20 - An object that is neutrally buoyant in salt water

A - Floats in fresh water too **B** - Sinks in fresh water

21 - An object weighs 20 kilograms and has a volume of 13 litres. What is its buoyancy in sea water?

A - 6.61 kilograms negative buoyancy **B** - 6.61 kilograms positive buoyancy

22 - How much weight you need to attach to an object of 12 kilograms that displaces 21 litres of seawater to make it 5 kilograms positively buoyant?

A - 9.63 kilograms **B** - 4.63 kilograms

23 - An object at the bottom of the sea weighs 30 kilograms and displaces 17 litres of water. How much air do you have to blow into a lift bag to make this object neutrally buoyant?

12.49 litres

12.13 litres

Physiology

1 - Cellular respiration produces

A - Carbon dioxide **B** - Carbon monoxide

2 - Carbon dioxide is mainly transported in the body by

A - Blood plasma **B** - Blood cells

3 - The substance that binds with oxygen in the blood cells is called

A - Haemoglobin **B** - Cellulose

4 - Blood low in oxygen looks

A - Bright red **B** - Dark red

5 - Carbon monoxide binds

A - 4 times more easily than oxygen with haemoglobin **B** - 200 times more easily than oxygen with haemoglobin

6 - Carbon monoxide poisoning causes

A - Hypoxia **B** - Blocking of arteries

7 - Arteries go

A - Towards the heart **B** - From the heart

8 - The artery that goes from the heart to the lungs is called

A - The aorta **B** - The pulmonary artery

9 - Arteries split up into smaller and smaller arteries. The smallest are called

A - The arterettes **B** - The capillaries

10 - The arteries in the neck are called

A - The carotid arteries **B** - The pulmonary arteries

11 - A tight hood may cause unconsciousness because

A - It block blood entering the brain **B** - It lowers the heart rate too much

12 - Bronchioles split into

A - Alveoli **B** - Trachea

13 - The breathing reflex is triggered by

A - Hypoxia **B** - Hypercapnia

14 - A shallow water black out is caused by

A - Dropping partial pressure of oxygen in the blood plasma **B** - Not hyperventilating enough

15 - Bradycardia is a part of the

A - The Mammalian reflex **B** - The consequences of hyperventilation

16 - Pulmonary oxygen toxicity is caused by

A - High partial pressure of oxygen **B** - Long exposure to high levels of oxygen

17 - Is pulmonary or central nervous system oxygen toxicity more dangerous?

A - Pulmonary **B** - Central nervous system

18 - All gases equally narcotic

A - TRUE **B** - FALSE

19 - Gas micronuclei are

A - Gas seeds **B** - The atoms that form a gas

Decompression Theory

1 - Tissues absorb nitrogen at different rates

A - TRUE **B** - FALSE

2 - After how many half times a tissue is considered to be full

A - 2 **B** - 6

3 - How full is a tissue after 3 half times

A - 87.5 percent **B** – Too much 150%

4 - If a tissue has a long half time it fills up

A - Slowly **B** - Quickly

5 - A compartment is another term for a

A - Theoretical tissue **B** - Pressure group

6 - Modern decompression tables are tested using

A - The occurrence of DCS **B** - The detection of silent bubbles

7 - All decompression models use the same letters for the same pressure groups

A - TRUE **B** - FALSE

8 - How many compartments does the US navy tables use

A - 6 **B** - 14

9 - How many metres of sea water pressure is there in a compartment with a half time of 60 minutes after 60 minutes at a depth of 15 meters seawater?

A - 7.5 msw **B** - 31 msw

10 - An M-value tells us how quickly a compartment fills up with nitrogen

A - TRUE **B** - FALSE

11 - Fast tissues have

A - High M-value **B** - Low M values

12 - A controlling compartment is a compartment that

A - Reaches its M-value first **B** - Is controlled by the theory

13 - Slow compartments reach their M value before fast compartments on

A - Long shallow dives **B** - Short deep dives

14 - Shallow dives are controlled by

A - Fast compartments **B** - Slow compartments

15 - To calculate surface intervals, tables like the US Navy and PADI RDP use a controlling compartment

A - TRUE **B** - FALSE

16 - The PADI RDP uses a

A - Compartment with a 60 minutes half time to calculate surface intervals **B** - Compartment with a 120 minutes half time to calculate surface intervals

17 - EE wash-out means that

A - The controlling compartment of the dive before is used to calculate surface intervals **B** - The exponential washout of fast tissues

Equipment

1 - Steel tanks are less buoyant than aluminium tanks

A - TRUE **B** - FALSE

2 - Aluminium tanks have higher working pressures than steel tanks

A - TRUE **B** - FALSE

3 - The safety valve on a scuba tank usually discharges the pressure in the tank when it get higher than

A - 160% of the working pressure **B** - 140% of the working pressure

4 - A visual inspection of the tank is recommended;

A - Every year **B** - Every 3-7 years, depending on local regulations

5 - Galvanic action takes place

A - Between the tank and the valve **B** - Inside the walls of the tank near the bottom

6 - During a hydrostatic test

A - The tank is pressurised to 160% of the working pressure **B** - The tank is pressurised to 180% of the working pressure

7 - A hydrostatic test uses

A - Air to pressurise the tank **B** - Water to pressurise the tank

8 - If a tank does not pass a hydrostatic test

A - It must be repaired **B** - It is destroyed

9 - If a tank has been too hot it should be hydrostatically tested. How hot?

A - 62 degrees Celsius **B** - 82 degrees Celsius

10 - The stamp "3AL" on a tank means that

A - The tank is made from steel **B** - The tank is made from aluminium

11 - What does "+" mean on a tank

A - That the tank is larger than usual **B** - That the tank can be filled to 110% of the working pressure

12 - A K-valve

A - Is screwed into the tank **B** - Is clamped over the tank

13 - Which valve is preferred in more demanding circumstances?

A - A DIN valve **B** - A J valve

14 - The first stage of a regulator

A - You attach to your tank **B** - You hold in your mouth

15 - In the first stage the pressure is reduced to ambient pressure

A - TRUE **B** - FALSE

16 - Intermediate pressure in regulators means

A - A pressure between the tank pressure and ambient pressure **B** - A pressure about 9 bar higher than ambient pressure

17 - An environmental seal in the first stage

A - Balances the regulator **B** - Makes it impossible for the first stage to freeze up in cold conditions

18 - A balanced regulator

A - Always maintains the same pressure, independent from demand **B** - Distributes the air supply evenly over the dive time

19 - A pilot valve is found in

A - The first stage **B** - The second stage

20 - An upstream valve opens

A - Against the air flow **B** - With the air flow

21 - The second stage of a regulator reduces the pressure by using the ambient pressure and a diaphragm

A - TRUE **B** - FALSE

22 - A failsafe regulator

A - Never fails **B** - Starts free flowing when something goes wrong

23 - A pilot valve is needed to open a bigger valve in

A - Upstream designs **B** - Downstream designs

24 - A venturi system works by

A - Disturbing the air flow in the second stage **B** - Opening a valve in the second stage

25 - At what percentage of oxygen do you have to use special equipment

A - 40% **B** - 50%

26 - A capillary depth gauge

A - Shows theoretical depths **B** - Shows absolute depths

27 - A bourdon type depth gauge

A - Is a tube that gets straighter the deeper you go **B** - Works with a small electrical current

28 - A transducer works with

A - Works with volume changes only **B** - Works with a small electrical current

Answer key.

The Dive environment	Physics	Physiology	Decompression	Equipment
01 B Moon	01 B 20 times	1 A Carbon Monoxide	1 A True	1 A True
02 B Semidiurnal	02 B conduction	2 B Blood plasma	2 B 6	2 B False
03 A Neap tide	03 A atoms bumping	3 A Haemoglobin	3 A	3 B 140%
04 A Clock wise	04 B Absorption	4 B Dark red	4 A slowly	4 A every year
05 B The Coriolis effect	05 A Diffusion	5 B 200 times	5 A theoretical tissue	5 A Tank and valve
06 B Cold water rising	06 A Cold water	6 A Hypoxia	6 B silent bubbles	6 A 160%
07 B Made by the sea	07 A four times faster	7 A	7 B False	7 B Water
08 B Crest to crest	08 B direction	8 B Pulmonary artery	8 A 6 compartments	8 B Destroyed
09 A Ripples	09 A 2.3 Bar	9 B Capillaries	9 A 7.5 msw	9 B 82 degrees
10 A True	10 A 3.62 Bar	10 A Carotid arteries	10 B False	10 Aluminium
11 B Constructive	11 B 4.71	11 B lowers heart rate	11 A high M values	11 110%
12 A maximum height	12 A 8 litres	12 A Alveoli	12 A M-value first	12 B clamped
13 B. 1.3 the height	13 A 4.18	13 B Hypercapnia..	13 Long shallow dive	13 A DIN valve
14 B some light	14 A 0.74	14 A Dropping pressure	14 B Slow Comp.	14 A tank
15 B Open ocean	15 A. 2.48	15 A Mammalian reflex	15 B False	15 B False
16 A Benthic	16 The PP is 1.05, yes	16 B Long exposure	16 A 60 minutes	16 B 9 bar higher
17 A living area	17 A 216.4	17 B CNS Toxicity	17 Controlling is surface	17 B Not freezing up
18 B Plankton	18 B Excessively	18 B False		18 A same pressure
19 A commensalism	19 A neutrally buoyant	19 A Gas seeds		19 B second stage
	20 B Sinks			20 A against air flow
	21 A 6.61 negative			21 A True
	22 B 4.63 kg			22 B Freeflow
	23 B 12.13 litres			23 A Upstream
				24 A disturbing air
				25 A 40%
				26 A Theoretical depths
				27 A A tube
				28 B Electrical current

TABLE OF FIGURES

Figure 1 Different gravity force of the moon on different places on earth

Figure 2 Two bulges of seawater caused by the gravity of the moon

Figure 3 Diurnal, semi-diurnal and mixed tides

Figure 4 Spring tides and neap tides caused by the sun and the moon

Figure 5 The Coriolis Effect

Figure 6 The main upwellings on earth

Figure 7 Wave form: height, length, speed, direction and frequency

Figure 8 Ripples, seas, and swells

Figure 9 Growing of wind waves in the fetch

Figure 10 Wave interference: constructive and destructive

Figure 11 Breaking waves in the surf

Figure 12 Zones in the ocean: Benthic, Pelagic; Euphotic, Disphotic and Aphotic

Figure 13 The ecosystem as a pyramid

Figure 14 Heat Movement: Conduction, Convection and Radiation

Figure 15 Refraction of light underwater

Figure 16 Turbidity and visual reversal

Figure 17 Absorption of light underwater

Figure 18 Pressure in salt water and fresh water, ambient, absolute and gauge pressure

Figure 19 A balloon at different depth, changes of volume and density

Figure 20 Bringing a balloon up and down to calculate the volume

Figure 21 Partial Pressure and depth

Figure 22 Pressure, Volume and Temperature of a gas

Figure 23 Saturation, super saturation and excessive super saturation

Figure 24 Buoyancy sum diagram

Figure 25 Aluminium and steel tanks

Figure 26 Markings on a tank

Figure 27 Tank valves

Figure 28 The first stage of regulator

Figure 29 The second stage of a regulator

Figure 30 Depth gauges

Figure 31 Haemoglobine at work in the blood

Figure 32 The heart

Figure 33 Arteries, capillaries, veins and gas exchange.

Figure 34 Blood pressure systole and diastole and heart contraction

Figure 35 Respiratory system, alveoli and pulmonary capillaries

Figure 36 Shallow water black out

Figure 37 The formation of bubbles

Figure 38 Decompression Sickness Type I and II and locations

Figure 39 Lung overexpansion injuries

Figure 40 The ear

Figure 41 Half times

Figure 42 Compartments and pressure in msw

Figure 43 Slow and fast compartments, and M-values

INDEX

absolute pressure 38
absorption 35
aluminium 56, 58
alveoli 74, 77, 79, 82, 83, 85, 88, 89, 90, 114
alveolus 74
ambient pressure 38
aphotic 25
apnea diving 76, 77
Arterial Gas Embolism (AGE) 90
artery 69
atrium 69
balanced first stage 61
baroreceptors 71
Barotraumas 89
benthic zone 25
bicarbonate 67
Blood 66
blue light 35
body temperature 95
Boyle's Law 39, 43, 111
bronchi 74, 79, 114
Bubble formation 82
bubbles 32, 49, 81, 82, 83, 84, 85, 86, 87, 88, 91, 112, 115
Buoyancy 50
burst disk 57
capillaries 70, 72, 74, 82, 88, 114
capillary depth gauge 63
capillary waves 21, 24, 110
carbon dioxide 66, 72, 74, 75, 76, 77, 78, 80, 113, 114
carbon monoxide 46, 66, 67, 68, 69, 112, 113
Carbon monoxide 46, 68, 69, 113
carbon monoxide poisoning 68, 69, 113
cardiovascular system 66, 69
carnivores 27
cellular respiration 66, 68, 113

Central Nervous System Oxygen Toxicity 79
chambers 69
Charles' Law 46
circulatory system 66, 72, 87, 95, 113
closed circuit rebreathers 60
Coasts 19
cochlea 92
commensalism 28
community 26, 29, 111
Compartments (theoretical tissues) 101
conduction 30
congestion 94
constructive interference 22
controlling compartment 104
convection 30
Coriolis Effect 17
Currents 15
Dalton's Law 43
decomposers 28
Decompression sickness 81, 83, 84
Decompression sickness type I 84
Decompression sickness type II 85
deep dives 77, 105, 108
density 36, 39, 43, 98, 111
depth gauge 63
destructive inference 22
diastolic blood pressure 71
diffusion 33
Digital depth gauges 64
DIN valve 58
disphotic 25
diurnal (daily) tides 13
Dive computers 107, 108
Doppler Ultrasound Flow Meter 82, 86, 115
Ear and sinus barotraumas 92
Ecology 26

ecosystem	26
EE washout model	108
equalise underwater	93
euphotic	25
Eustachian tube	94
Eustachian Tube	93
extended surface interval	108
fast tissues	100, 101, 104
fetch	21
float	50
food chain	28
food web	28, 29, 111
freak waves	23
free diving	76
Frenzel manoeuvre	93
Fully Developed Sea	22
galvanic action	57
gas micronuclei	81, 86, 115
Gas narcosis	80, 81, 115
gas seeds	81
Gauge pressure	38
gravity of the Moon and the Sun	10
habitat	26
haemoglobin	66, 68, 113
half-times	98, 99, 102, 104
Half-times	98
heat exhaustion	95, 96
heat stroke	95, 96
heat transmission	30
Helium	80
herbivores	27
hood	71
hydrostatic test	57, 58
hypercapnia	75, 76, 77, 78, 80, 114
Hyperoxia	75, 78, 114
hyperthermia	95, 96
hyperventilate	77, 78, 114
hypocapnia	75, 78, 114
hypothermia	95, 96
hypoxia	68, 71, 75, 77, 78, 114
immune system	82
inner ear	92, 94
interference	22
J-valve	58
Lung expansion injuries	89
lungs	74
major ocean currents	17
major winds	15
mammalian reflex	77, 78, 114
Mediastinal emphysema	91
micro bubbles	81, 82, 86, 115
micronuclei	81, 86, 87, 115
middle ear	92, 93, 94
mixed tides	13
mutualism	28
M-value	104, 105, 108
neap tide	15
negative buoyancy	50, 54, 112
neutral buoyancy	50, 54, 112
nitrogen	44, 46, 66, 78, 80, 81, 82, 83, 85, 86, 87, 88, 98, 104, 108, 112, 115
nitrogen narcosis	80
nitrogen pressure	98, 102
Nitrox	45, 46, 79, 80, 112, 115
nosebleed	94
off-gas	87, 108
open circuit scuba	60
open or closed bourdon tube	64
operational pressure	56, 57
outer ear	92
oxygen	44, 46, 66, 67, 68, 69, 72, 74, 75, 77, 78, 79, 80, 85, 87, 88, 90, 91, 111, 113, 114, 115
oxygen clean	63
PADI RDP	101, 102, 107, 108
parasitism	28, 29, 111
Patent Foramen Ovale (PFO)	83

127

patterns of tides	13
pelagic zone	25
phytoplankton	27
plasma	66, 68, 77, 78, 85, 113, 115
Pneumothorax or collapsed lung	91
population	26
positive buoyancy	50, 54, 112
Pressure	37, 38, 44, 89
pressure gradient	81, 86, 88, 98, 115
primary coasts	19
primary producers	27
pulmonary artery	70
pulmonary decompression sickness	85
Pulmonary Oxygen Toxicity	79
radiation	30, 32, 111
red blood cells	66, 68, 85, 113
refraction	32
regulator first stage	60
regulator second stage	62
Repetitive dives	107
reverse block	94
ripples	21
risk of decompression sickness	66, 85, 86, 104, 115
Risk of decompression sickness	86
rogue waves	23
round window	93
safety valve	57
saturation	49
seas	21
second stage	61, 62
secondary coasts	19
semi-closed circuit	60
semi-diurnal (that means half-daily) tides	13
shallow dives	105
shallow water black-out	77
silent bubbles	82, 86, 115
sink	50, 53, 54, 112
sinuses	94

slow tissues	100, 104
species	26
speed of sound under water	36
spinning Earth	16
spring tide	15
steel	56, 58
Subcutaneous emphysema	91
super-saturation	48, 49, 86, 115
surf	23
swells	21
symbiotic relationships	28
systolic blood pressure	71
Tanks	56
temperature change	47, 48, 112
theoretical tissues	98, 101, 102
tidal waves,	19, 24, 110
Tides	10
trachea	74, 79, 114
Trimix	80
unbalanced first stage	61
upwellings	18
urge to breath	75, 78, 114
US Navy tables	102, 107, 108
Valsalva	93
vasodilatation	95, 96
vein	69
ventricle	69
Venturi valve	62
vestibular canal	92
visual inspection	57, 63
Visual reversion	34
Volume	40
wash-out	108
wave frequency	20, 24, 110
wave height	20, 24, 110
wave length	20
wave propagation	20, 24, 110
wave speed	20, 24, 110

Waves 19	yoke valve 58
wind pipe 74	zooplankton 27
wind waves 19	zooxanthellae 28
working pressure 56, 57, 58	

Printed in Great Britain
by Amazon